It Takes
Two
To Tangle

PHILIP WIEBE

It Takes Two To Tangle

Treading Lightly Through the Ties and Binds of Relationships

WINNIPEG, MANITOBA

HILLSBORO, KANSAS

Published simultaneously by Kindred Productions. Winnipeg, Manitoba R2L 2E5 and Kindred Productions, Hillsboro, Kansas 67063.

All Scripture quotations, unless otherwise indicated, are taken from the HOLY BIBLE NEW INTERNATIONAL VERSION®. NIV®. Copyright © 1973, 1978, 1984 by International Bible Society. Used by permission of Zondervan Publishing House. All rights reserved. Other versions used include: the New Living Translations [NLT], copyright © 1996, used by permission of Tyndale House Publishers, Inc. Wheaton, Illinois 60189; The Living Bible [TLB] copyright © 1971, used by permission of Tyndale House Publishers, Inc. Wheaton, Illinois, 60189 and the King James Version [KJV].

Book and cover design by Fred Koop, Winnipeg, MB.
Printed by The Christian Press, Winnipeg, MB.

Canadian Cataloguing in Publication Data

Wiebe, Philip,   1958-

   It takes two to tangle

   ISBN: 0-921788-58-4

Man-woman relationships—Religious aspects—
Christianity.   2. Man-woman relationships—Religous
aspects—Christianity—Humor.   I. Title

BV4597.52.W53   1999   248.8 ' 44 ' 0207   C99-920211-1

International Standard Book Number: 0-921788-58-4

Contents

Introduction

In the overly studied, endlessly discussed world of modern relationships, I've often thought that one way we could take our own relationships more seriously would be to take them a little less seriously. How strange that in an era of unprecedented research and education, many of society's defining relationships—marriage, family, community, church—seem more fragile and endangered than ever before. Or maybe it isn't so strange. Perhaps it's simply what happens when we spend more time talking and thinking about relationships than actually being in relationship.

That's why I wonder if we've become too serious about relationships to really take them seriously. We hold them at arm's length to examine and scrutinize, then hesitate to get any closer for fear of what might happen next. And despite all the studies and surveys and research, you still can't predict the ways of the human heart. If you could, where would the fun be? This modern tendency to plan every moment of our day and our life can cut off the very ties (and binds) that make relationships most rewarding. A true knitting of hearts can't happen in a few easy steps or a few minutes a day.

Amid the tangles that occur when real people try to get along in real life, one of the great relationship enhancers is laughter. I don't mean laughing at each other. We suffer through more than enough of that these days.

Better is laughing with each other—and at ourselves. These put into practice the Bible's recommendation that we "not think more highly of ourselves than we ought." Nothing hinders relationships more effectively than today's common practice of thinking much of one's self and little of anyone else.

Humor has enjoyed a growing reputation in recent years as an aid to recovery, connection and healthful living. It has even made strides in Christianity, which has never exactly been known for levity. Many years ago my own church denomination even passed a resolution "that jesting and joking by our brethren verbally or in writing, in conversation or in published periodicals should be desisted from."

That may (fittingly) seem amusing now, but I understand the intent. We want to take God and each other seriously. Yet I think we're learning that being serious can—and should—have a lighter side. When we humans take ourselves more seriously than we take God, the trouble starts.

By kidding modern gender and relationship issues, I suppose I'm trying to stir up the trouble before it solidifies at the bottom. In other words, laughing about our faults and foibles now can help us avoid becoming rigid and inflexible later. After all, we don't want to be the ones future generations smile at for issuing the "No Smiling" rule. In relationships, as in all of life, a little joy today can save a lot of woe tomorrow.

PART ONE

Men and Women

Relation-Ships that Pass in the Night

Closing the Gap

There is an amazing amount of research being conducted these days about the state of modern relationships. Studies and surveys and magazine quizzes plumb the depths of men's and women's feelings toward each other. Authors and speakers and relationship experts pour over endless details of gender issues. The monumental results of all these efforts, according to the experts, can be summed up in a profound new relationship theory: Men and women are different.

I thought so. In fact, I've suspected it for years. By second grade, for instance, I began to notice that a certain girl named Valerie was inexplicably more attractive than any of my guy friends. I responded to this realization, naturally, by avoiding her like the plague. Eventually I grew out of this and sought to be closer to certain females, who, in turn, avoided me like the plague.

Little did I realize that I was ahead of my time. It seems that the wiser, more sensitive, more sophisticated humanity becomes, the more men and women want to avoid each other as much as humanly possible.

The notion that women are from Venus and men are from Mars not only echoes a best-selling book title, it also reflects conventional wisdom on the current state of male-female relationships. Gender gaps are in. Since guys and gals come from vastly different worlds, the thinking goes, we shouldn't even try to understand each other. We just need to learn enough alien traits and code words to get a date, coexist with a colleague, make points with a boss, keep peace with a spouse, and so on—at least until the rocket ships come to whisk us all back to our home planets.

Perhaps I exaggerate. Still, a popular concept circulating these days is that the genders are "wired" differently. Why, for example, do social gatherings often deteriorate into isolated clots of women and men who snort and chortle about the irrationality and hopelessness of the opposite gender? It must be in the wiring. Cross your wires and *zap*, people get burned.

Though the evidence is mounting against me, I'm not ready to concede that women and men should live their lives on separate circuits. Many people seem to believe that learning to get along with your spouse requires getting away from your spouse to be taught about the opposite gender by people of your own gender. I, on the other hand, believe that men and women can actually learn things from each other. And not just by attending gender-specific conferences and rallies, but by spending time with each other. Really. I know it's a radical concept, but allow me to illustrate.

It has sometimes been generalized that a man views his car as an extension of himself, whereas a woman views her car as an extension of her purse. Assuming for a moment this to be true, who would you say is right? With apologies to the guy who once bragged to me that he paid $89,000 for his car (upon which I was tempted to ask how many bathrooms it came with) I have to go with the woman. When you think about it, a car is little more than a purse with wheels—a big container to haul stuff around in. Men who believe that cars can enhance their "image" might want to think hard about identifying themselves so intimately with something that is full of gas and has a spare tire.

It has also been said that men go to the store *when* they need to buy something, whereas women go to the store to see *if* they need to buy something. Here I have to stick with men. There is something strange about the notion of "recreational shopping"—sort of like "aerobic channel-surfing." Once, while I was waiting as my wife tried on jeans, I saw a woman rush up to a designer pantsuit hanging on a rack. She bowed reverently before it, examining the material, and exclaimed, "Oh my *god!*" *Yes*, I thought, *perhaps it is.*

Another generalization that has been made is that women read, while men watch. I don't mean men watch women read, I mean they watch TV, movies, video games and sports contests, while many women could take or leave these spectacles and would rather read a good book. I give my nod to women. Not to disparage the video arts, which can be very entertaining and informative, but in my experience 20 minutes reading a book is far more satisfying to mind and soul than any three hours watching, say, a football game. And I like football. Once I read an article (by a man) arguing that "smart women like to watch sports," but if you ask me, women are smart to avoid watching sports. And here's proof: A clever guy I know decided to tape an entire football game to see how much of it was actual game rather than commercials, babbling sportscasters, time-outs, penalties, huddles and whatnot. The grand total: 20 minutes.

It has also been said that men tend to ignore dirt while women obsess over it. Obviously one needs to stay within reason here, but I think men have a point. Don't get me wrong—I firmly believe men and women should pitch in together to keep their homes clean, organized and friendly. But we're not making computer chips here. Keeping homes laboratory-spotless—following guests around with a Dustbuster and assaulting every stray germ with Lysol—is hardly compatible with family fun and fellowship. Fortunately many modern women have broken free from the cleaning-frenzy syndrome that once pervaded the land. Some equate that with the fall of Civilization As We Know It, but if unrealistic domestic perfection is the standard, I say let it fall.

For a long time it has seemed to me that men have tended to vote with issues and women with persons. I go with women. Once when someone was trying to convince me to vote for a certain candidate, I objected. The candidate had a sketchy record of personal and financial indiscretions as well as reneged campaign promises. "So?" my friend responded. "You have to go with the issues." I'm not so sure. If candidates don't care about their own issues as much as they care about getting elected, what's the point in voting for them in the first place? Many women I've known have seemed more willing than men to vote for persons with whom they may disagree on some issues, but who display consistent integrity and compassion.

In some things, I've noticed, women tend to think conceptually and men chronologically. For example, when my wife tells a story or describes an event, she often starts in the middle and jumps all over the map, while I invariably go from beginning to end. I'm not saying one way is better than the other (my wife's stories, in fact, are usually more entertaining than mine), but there is one area where the nod goes to the chronological male: household projects. Rome couldn't be built in a day. Neither can a deck. It is not unheard of that a woman will say to her mate, "Let's remodel the kitchen!" "Hmm," replies the man, "by when were you thinking?" "Well," she says, "we have guests coming tomorrow night."

A final common observation is that men conquer, while women relate. Do I really need to say that women have the better angle here? I know the manly man has made a comeback, marching around making a name for himself and protecting his brood. But conquering isn't always such a good thing. For every genuine achievement, discovery or exploration of some new frontier men have accomplished, there are numerous examples of the kind of conquering that involves death, oppression, exploitation, environmental devastation.

Some may still protest, "Would we be where we are today if throughout history men sat around talking instead of going out and kicking some butt?"

To which I answer, my point exactly.

I could go on. It seems obvious to me, though, that men and women are better off sticking together than drifting apart. We're more alike than many care to admit these days. We are all made in God's image, and are all one in Christ. And perhaps most important in our gender-divided time, we are encouraged to look out not only for our own needs, but also for the needs of the other.

That's the hard part. The world tells us to look out for number one, but the Bible reminds us of a profound old relationship theory: Number one is the other one.

Communication
Complications

A great ongoing opportunity for women and men to encourage and learn from each other is in the home. Marriage is the closest kind of partnership. Spouses find strength in each other's abilities. They gain wisdom from each other's perspectives. They deepen their spiritual lives as a result of each other's prayers and devotional insights. And the key to all of this, as the relationship experts tell us time and time again, is maintaining good communication.

Unfortunately, I haven't gotten around to communicating that with my wife yet. I don't think I've actually seen her since the day before yesterday. I know she still lives here, though, because occasionally I observe a brunette blur flying by or notice a familiar shape sleeping on the left side of the bed in the middle of the night. Maybe it isn't quite that bad, but sometimes it seems that way. The more Kim and I try to communicate, it seems, the more persistent the distractions become.

Work... When people find out I work from a home office, many exclaim, "You're so lucky!" Well, it is true that I enjoy the good fortune of being able to strike up a conversation with my lovely wife at any time, in a manner similar to the following:

Me: "Hon, I wanted to tell you how much I..."

Phone: Riiing...

Me: "Hold on a second... Hello?"

Person on phone: "Thank goodness you're there! I need you to send me the..."

Fax: Beeeep...

Me: "Hold on a second... Kim, could you get that fax? Now, you were saying you need me to send you the..."

Computer: "You have mail..."

Me: "Hold on a second, I need to check my e-mail... OK, you were saying you need me to..."

Person on phone: "Just a minute, I need to answer my other line (click)."

Me: "All right Hon, now that I have a moment I want to tell you how much I..."

Home phone: Riiing...

Kim: "Hold on a second, I'd better get this..."

And so it goes. Except on the days Kim goes off to work, of course. On those days I hardly get one call, and could strike up a conversation with my lovely wife at any time.

Home... Another great advantage of working from a home office, besides the ability to strike up a conversation with my lovely wife at any time, is the fact that I can be present when pipes burst or major appliances break down. That always starts a lively conversation, with relationship-deepening declarations such as "Not again," and "How much will *that* cost?" At these times we are convinced we can hear our house giggling with glee in the background, smug in the knowledge that it has sabotaged yet another potential "relationship moment." When our realtor said this house had personality, we had no idea he meant it literally.

Church... Since our church is very committed to encouraging marital communication, we occasionally get flyers that read something like this:

Relationship Conference
Get away from your spouse for the weekend to learn more about getting along with your spouse!

We'll hustle you off right after work on Friday and get you home late Saturday night so you'll have no actual time to put anything you learned into practice. Plus, your mate will likely be less than pleased that you left him or her alone to handle the parenting, housework and kids activities with no help at all. And as an added bonus, we'll give tips on how to schedule even more monthly meetings and support groups so you can enjoy the benefits of getting away from your spouse to learn more about getting along with your spouse all year long!

Perhaps the flyers don't really say that, but maybe they should. Sometimes I think church-issued flyers and bulletins would benefit from the occasional warning label related to today's overabundance of rallies and meetings and seminars: "Caution—You may not really need to attend this relationship conference. You may just need to stay home for a change, turn off the TV and simply sit there on the sofa holding your spouse's hand." That's the kind of meeting we married couples could stand to attend more often.

Kids... While I humbly admit that my two young children are the most adorable human beings in the history of the universe, they do sometimes make marital intimacy a bit of a challenge. When we want to know our children's whereabouts, for instance, all Kim and I need to do is sit down on the sofa and say, "We finally have a few minutes to chat." Instantly, of course, our kids will rush in and dive on top of us.

Kim and I will try to talk anyway. "Mommy," one child will say, sensing that we might be starting to have a meaningful conversation. "Shh," Mommy will reply. "Daddy and I are talking right now."

Said child will nod understandingly and say, "Mommy MommyMommyMommyMommyMommyMommyMommyMommyMommyMommyMommyMommy..."

At which point other child will chime in, "DaddyDaddyDaddyDaddyDaddyDaddyDaddyDaddyDaddyDaddyDaddyDaddyDaddyDaddyDaddyDaddy..."

In order to hear each other, Mommy's and Daddy's voices will continue to rise in volume, along with the increasing amplification of the children's voices, until the moment when the Air National Guard may have to warn that their radars have detected an unusually powerful ground disturbance at the exact location of our house. Either that, or the kids will suddenly become absolutely silent at the precise moment one of us is shouting details of an embarrassing incident: "I SNEEZED JUICE ALL OVER THE GUEST PASTOR AT OUR BIG PRAYER BREAKFAST."

The children, it goes without saying, will find this to be the most hilarious thing ever said since the beginning of time. They will laugh for hours, then repeat the juice-sneezing incident to every houseguest, fellow church member and random passerby they come across for months. Mommy and Daddy will have to go into hiding.

Maybe then we'll get a chance to talk. But of course once we try, the kids will rush in—even if we're holed up at a remote mountain monastery in Tibet—and dive on top of us.

Progress... The only thing more effective than kids at interrupting a conversation is technology. We have way too many beeping devices in our home. Those TVs and stereos and computers and cell phones and pagers and answering machines and microwave ovens and so on, allegedly designed to make our lives easier, all seem to conspire against us when it comes to getting a word in edgewise. When Kim and I sit down to have a chat, they all seem to call, "Watch me, answer me, listen to me, play with me, pay attention to me." It isn't easy to resist.

Still, there are times when Kim and I simply need to ignore our entertainment and communication devices and determine to have real live conversation. So we sit down, make ourselves comfortable and launch out into bold new territory.

"Tell me," Kim will say. "How has everything been going? What new things have you been learning? What insights have you been gleaning from your devotions? Have you been praying for me and the kids?"

To which I will respond, in all honesty and earnestness, "Is that the phone?"

Mr. Sensitive meets Mr. Macho

Another communication complication that can come up between men and women is the fact that modern "relationship rules" keep changing. Gender-related roles, trends and expectations continue to shift with unsettling frequency. A few years ago, for example, I noticed a newspaper article stating that after years of neglect, macho manhood was making a comeback. That was news to me. Reflecting back, I can imagine an interesting series of events that news article might have initiated...

"Says here," I told my wife from behind the paper one evening, "that sensitive guys are out."

She replied, "You mean they were in?"

I lowered the paper. "Sure," I said. "Don't you remember a few years ago when the media reported that Sensitivity Boom?"

"Guess I didn't hear it," Kim said. "Maybe I was vacuuming."

I gave her a look, but all I could see was the back of her novel. "Anyway," I continued, "the sensitive man is history, *outré*, *passé*. You gals have decided you like macho men better."

"Really?" Kim inquired, lowering her novel. "Too bad."

"I don't know," I said. "Maybe our muddle-headed world could use a dose of manly ..."

"I mean," Kim interrupted, "too bad I didn't marry a macho man."

I'm sure I don't have to tell you that hurt a little. Sure, I'd gotten stuck in the sensitivity muck for awhile, but it wasn't too late to change. If women liked macho men, my woman was going to get a macho man.

Now I only had to figure out what it was, exactly, that macho men did.

It wasn't long before I gathered, from the hallowed TV ad authorities, that macho men took off their shirts a lot. I decided to try it.

Kim looked stunned when I walked into the room one afternoon without my shirt. "What...are...you..."

I must say it pleased me that my shirtless torso sent her so aflutter. Affecting a manly scowl, I sauntered towards her and...

"Are you out of your mind?" Kim cried. "It's Sunday dinner!"

That was, I suppose, a point to ponder. But there wasn't much time to ponder it after elderly Mrs. Goolahee, who was over for dinner, strolled into the room and immediately became flushed and weak in the knees. I might even have taken that as a compliment had she not been laughing uncontrollably at the time.

Maybe taking off my shirt didn't give off the macho aura I was looking for. Soon after, I learned from a manly neighbor with a tattoo that macho men didn't do girly stuff like wash dishes and change diapers. As one who'd done far too many dishes and diapers, I looked for a chance to take my stand.

"Got to get to my meeting," Kim said one evening, handing me the baby as she left. "She needs changing."

"Well, woman," I growled, "I don't do diapers no more."

Kim squinted at me for a second, then shrugged and said, "Suit yourself."

I would, thank you. Sniff. Yep, no diaper changing for me. Cough. Little odor never hurt anyone. Gag. Okay punkin, why don't you play on the other side of the room for awhile? Let go of my shirt, hon, I just want to...say, how'd I get this smear of chocolate on my...*eeeewww!*

So much for not changing diapers. Not long after it

dawned on me the sure sign of machodumb, er, machodom was a tool belt. Manly men fixed things. That seemed like a couldn't-loose proposition. I got to jangle around with flashy tools and the little woman got stuff around the house fixed.

When I jangled into the kitchen one Saturday with hammers and wrenches and wire cutters dangling from my belt, Kim looked at me suspiciously and said, "What are you doing?"

"Gonna fix that there hoven fan hain't bin warkin'."

"Huh?"

"Uh, oven fan needs fixing."

"We already have an electrician coming."

"No wimpy ee-lectrician gonna touch my fan. I'm a man, and a man fixes hisself. Er, fixes *things* hisself."

Without another word Kim dialed the phone and said, "Emergency? I'd like to report a fire."

Heh, heh. The little kidder.

Looking back on it, though, it was pretty amazing how the fire trucks roared up at the exact moment the fire started. I mean, I almost had the fan fixed when *wooom*, these sparks shot out of the oven hood and receded my hairline a bit prematurely.

I thought Kim's glare was a tad severe. "Don't worry," I soothed. "My hair will grow back."

She covered her face and let out a whimper. Maybe her hay fever was acting up. When the firefighters filed in, Kim uncovered her face and said, "Husband fixed something." They nodded gravely, understanding all.

Maybe tools weren't my thing, but there were other ways I could be handy. I'd once heard a macho friend brag that he had never let one of those effeminate express lube joints with free gourmet coffee change the oil in his car. He always did it himself. Even *I*, I thought, could replace old oil with new. I'd done it in the popcorn maker plenty of times.

I headed for the auto parts store and asked for some oil-changing tips. The clerk explained the procedure and concluded, "Be sure to check the oil level when you're done."

"With what?" I asked.

The clerk grinned at me and said, "Dipstick."

I admit I was an oil-changing novice, but I think he was out of line to insult me like that.

With a bit of trial and error I did get my oil changed. I sauntered inside to tell Kim the good news. She gave a look of genuine surprise and commented, "YAAA!" So maybe I did dribble a small pool of Penzoil on the linoleum. No reason to get all worked up.

After the oil-changing slip-up—as I tried to leave the kitchen I slipped ten feet on the oil and took out a small utility shelf—I decided my best chance at constructive machoness would be to take a more active role as the protector of my woman and the fruit of my looms, er, loins. My big chance came as I arrived home one evening at dusk. A suspicious looking character seemed to be sneaking in the front door. I jumped onto the porch with a tire iron and yelled, "FREEZE!"

When she came to I tried to tell Kim's mom I was sorry, but noooo. Kim kept going on about checking if insanity ran in my family.

Later she asked, "What were you thinking?"

I took her demure, fragile hand and soothed, "Just a routine mistake in my role as manly protector of the weaker sex."

She snapped back her hand and, while I was feeling to see if my arm was still in its socket, said, "So. Who in this room besides me has recently delivered two kids after eighteen months of heavy pregnancy, thirty hours of hard labor and one major surgery?"

I didn't see any hands go up.

"Well then. Who else devotes full time to developing these wonderful, complicated, trying little fireballs into responsible human beings while still finagling time for personal growth and volunteer service?"

Still no hands.

"And who else still manages to fit in a job assisting in eye surgery not for money or prestige, Lord knows, but simply to save people's sight and help them have a better life?"

So she helped with eye surgery. I could have done that, provided I could have kept my own eyes closed.

"Is there anyone in this room," Kim concluded, "you'd care to call 'the weaker sex'?"

I decided to refrain from pointing at Kim. Getting clobbered by the weaker sex wouldn't have looked good for my macho image...

So, looking back, it's probably a good thing I never followed through on the small macho impulse stirred up by that newspaper article I mentioned earlier. Any real attempt to get manlier, I think, could have put me in the hospital.

Surviving Surefire Romance

Sometimes I wonder if another good way to end up in the hospital is by seeking romance. At least the contemporary version. It seems that the kind of romantic endeavors portrayed by many of today's novels and movies and magazines, if pursued in real life, could get people hurt. In the case of my wife and I, in fact, it almost did.

But before I get to that, let me say that I find the modern romantic ideal to be rather intriguing. Romance has been around for centuries, but not necessarily with the expectation that it should be high on the priority lists of longtime married couples. Surely Depression-era folks, for example, had no extra time or money to spend on regular date nights and romantic getaways. We modern couples, by contrast, have no extra time or money to spend on regular date nights and romantic getaways either, but we do them anyway. Which may be why, as compared to Depression-era folks, we seem to be a lot more depressed these days.

But romance is here to stay, so we may as well grin and bear it. So to speak. With so many great ideas out there for getting more romance into our marriages, the only real problem we face is that there are so many great ideas out there for getting more romance into our marriages. When romance experts grace us with the latest surefire ways to fan the flames of passion, there is only one reasonable way to respond. Run.

Which is actually what I had to do one time, early in my marriage, after following a romance article's advice to surprise Kim with a cozy fireside dinner at home. How suave I felt, sneaking home early to set up a candle-lit table, put on soft music and prepare a gourmet meal. To which Kim responded, when she came home, by fainting right into a coma. OK, not really—but she did swoon with delight and glide off to change into "something more comfortable"—sweats and a ratty T-shirt. When we snuggled into our chairs and popped open a bottle of sparkling cider, the sparks really started flying.

Literally. *Chimney Fire!*

I'm not making this up. That our cranky old woodstove chose that moment to spit flames out of the stovepipe was, of course, purely a matter of chance. A chance, that is, for the romance experts to roll on the floor laughing. And possibly the firefighters too. When the flames appeared I bolted out the front door and raced to our local fire station, which fortunately was only 50 yards away at the end of our block. As the firefighters traipsed in and noticed our romantically ap-pointed table next to the wood stove, I'm sure I wit-nessed no shortage of sly grins and muffled guffaws.

For me that incident raises the question: Should we couples who can barely back out of the driveway with-out knocking over garbage cans be expected to ad-vance the dance of romance like Fred Astaire and Gin-ger Rogers? I'm not so sure. About that time I also ex-perienced another run-in with the "dance of romance" when I, the ultimate non-dancer, agreed to chance a slow-dance with Kim at a wedding reception. "Nobody will notice us," she assured me. Until a couple of weeks later, it turned out, when the wedding video was issued. There I was, prominently featured in the recep-tion footage, captured for all time as the ultimate argu-ment in favor of mandatory dance lessons.

It seems to me that this is what happens when fanta-sy romance is attempted by a certain cultural element, meaning real people. The problem is that real-life at-tempts at romance, unlike the neatly plotted variety found in popular literature and media, can lead to real-life consequences:

Suggested Action: Scatter fresh-cut flowers all over the master bedroom.

Real Reaction: Exhausted spouse flops on bed, inciting passionate trip to emergency room to have several dozen rose thorns removed from posterior.

Suggested Action: Go out for an intimate evening at a trendy new eatery.

Real Reaction: Spouse severely disagrees that formal attire was necessary for grand opening of Taco Bell.

Suggested Action: Compose a romantic poem sharing innermost feelings.

Real Reaction: Spouse not moved by "Roses are red/Violets are violet./I love you enough/To put the lid down on the toilet."

Suggested Action: Whisk spouse away for relaxing weekend out of town.

Real Reaction: Spouse somewhat miffed to be whisked away while you stay home and watch TV.

The point is that surefire romance is often overrated as a marriage enhancer, while simpler relational concepts—such as not talking with your mouth full—are consistently undervalued. That may sound silly, but small things like table manners go a lot further toward promoting marital bliss than you might think. Surveys keep showing that elaborate romantic encounters aren't really what longtime mates desire most of all—what they really want are more back rubs. This is certainly true at my house. Whenever I give my wife a back rub after a hard day, she will soon be fluttering her eyelashes at me and whispering softly into my ear, right there on the sofa, that sweet nothing every spouse loves to hear: "*zzzzzzzz...*"

But I don't mind. What gets us modern married couples most excited, I think, is beautiful boredom. Who has time to scheme up all this complicated stuff like putting together a romantic candle-lit chimney fire? Many couples today aren't looking for more excitement, but more sleep. Believe me, with kids and jobs and church responsibilities and housework and after-school activities and a dozen other things to look after, most couples already experience about as much excitement as they can stand.

I don't mean we should abandon romance, but I do think we should realize that true romance starts with the little stuff. Like helping with the dishes. Or giving your mate more than 24-hour notice that the house has to be completely repainted before the in-laws show up. Or not inviting your golfing buddies over for dinner the day your spouse had her wisdom teeth pulled and resembles a drooling Sharpei puppy. You'd think married couples would instinctively know this, but it's amazing how often these kinds of foul-ups occur. No wonder novels and movies and magazines get so much mileage out of fantasy romance these days. It takes spouses' minds off the fact that in real life, they may rarely get a moment's consideration.

Perhaps the time is right, then, to tone down the fantasy romance and put more effort into reality romance. Here are a few places to start:

Suggested Action: Stack freshly cleaned and folded laundry in the master bedroom.

Real Reaction: Spouse can suddenly dance like Fred Astaire or Ginger Rogers at the prospect of not having to do laundry for the eighth day in a row.

Suggested Action: Go out for an uneventful evening at a trashy old eatery.

Real Reaction: Spouse eternally grateful that he or she doesn't have to change out of sweats and ratty T-shirt.

Suggested Action: Avoid reciting bad romantic poetry.

Real Reaction: Spouse would rather hear a simple "I love you" anyway.

Suggested Action: Whisk the kids away for a relaxing day out of town.

Real Reaction: Just the kids. You two stay home. Do I need to draw a picture?

I've joked about a few of the romance mistakes my wife and I have made over the years, but there is one thing I think we got right from the very beginning. When we were planning our wedding day years ago, people kept offering advice on how to make it the most important, most memorable, most romantic event of our lives. Finally one of us said what we both were thinking: "I don't see this as the most important day of our lives, but only as the beginning of our life together."

Now that was romantic. And we've tried to be so ever since. What I mean, of course, is that we give a lot of back rubs.

I Could Be Right, But Don't Hold Your Breath

One of the great gender debates of our day has to do with who's right. Women or men? There is a certain male faction that apparently would like to take us back to an earlier age, when men were right and women were quiet. Men were in charge, in other words, and women were the help. Returning to this golden social structure would solve all our problems, the argument goes. Families would stay together, children would stay off the streets, unemployment would decline, and most important of all, guys would be free once again to play golf on Saturday mornings rather than having to help around the house.

Probably the stronger feeling that persists today, however, is that women are right. Men have messed up the world long enough, many contend, with their misplaced aggression and improper laundry-folding techniques. Now is the time for women to step forward and claim their rightful places as the true brains behind the project of life. Or at least get their proper due for being right about everything.

Though my moderate nature argues against it, there have been times, I have to admit, when I've wondered if women *are* always right. If I were to have a conversation about that with my imaginary liberal friend Skip T. Cull, it might go something like this...

"I'm not sure how it is with you," I commented to Skip one afternoon at a backyard barbecue, "but sometimes it seems that my wife always has to be right about everything."

Rather than getting the response I was expecting—the knowing male eye-roll—Skip replied, "Well, maybe she is."

That stunned me for a moment. Finally I said, "Thanks for giving me credit."

"Oh, no," Skip responded, "I didn't mean that personally. I meant that in general, women are always right."

I should have guessed he'd think that, being an unashamed liberal and supporter of feminism. Still, it rankled me. "How can you say that?" I asked.

"OK," Skip said, "say you're trying to get somewhere you've never been and can't quite find it. What would you do?"

I wasn't sure what Skip was getting at, but played along. "Obviously," I said, "I'd keep looking until I find it."

"And what would your wife say to do?"

With a short laugh, I replied, "My wife would say, and I quote, 'Stop and ask that guy for directions.'"

Skip said, "And who would be right?"

"Well, I don't think you could say anyone would be right or wrong in that situation, because it's just two different approaches to…"

"Let's see," Skip interrupted. "On the one hand you say to keep looking, which will get you there an hour late with steam shooting out your ears. On the other hand Kim says stop and ask for directions, which will take all of 30 seconds and get you there on time, stress free. Who's right?"

I felt my face getting warm as I stammered, "Er, um, well…"

"I thought so. Now here's another one. Somebody gives you courtside playoff tickets, but the game is on the same night as your son's small role as a supporting carrot in the "Clean Teeth are Happy Teeth" pageant. What do you do?"

"That's a tough one," I said thoughtfully. "I mean, it isn't every day someone gives you courtside playoff tickets, so I suppose you'd have to weigh the…"

"What would your wife say?"

I was starting to get that sinking feeling that often plagued me when talking with Skip. "She'd say," I admitted reluctantly, 'Basketball games are nice, but how often is your son a supporting carrot in the "Clean Teeth are Happy Teeth" pageant? It'll seem like next week when he's graduating from college, so you'd better enjoy his childhood now.'"

Skip nodded somberly and said, "Women are always right. Think about it."

I did, and frankly it didn't sit well with me. I decided to put Skip's theory to the test. Kim would be getting the eye of scrutiny from me for awhile, I could tell you that.

And I thought I had her right away. We'd done a little shopping and Kim had exclaimed at the store, "This skirt would go perfectly with my olive blazer!" A few days later when she was going to wear the combination, however, she said, "Maybe I don't like this skirt after all. Guess I'll take it back."

In retrospect, I probably shouldn't have hollered "AHA!" quite so enthusiastically. Kim jumped about three feet off the carpet and yelped, "What did you do *that* for?"

"Uh, sorry," I replied. "I was just thinking that a few days ago you said you'd found the perfect skirt."

"So?"

"Now you're going to take it back."

She gave me that look that said, "And your point, if in fact you have one, is...?"

"I guess you were wrong. About the skirt, I mean."

Kim mulled that over a moment, then said, "I believe my exact words were, 'This skirt would go perfectly with my olive blazer.' Which it does. However, it turns out I don't like the way it fits."

"So buying it was a mistake," I pronounced a little too smugly. "You don't find us men returning stuff to the store all the time like you women do."

"That's true," Kim said. "You prefer to have something hang uselessly in the closet for the rest of your life because it doesn't fit or there's something 'weird' about it, to use your word, whereas I keep the receipt and with no hesitation whatsoever trade it in for something I do like."

I opened my mouth for rebuttal but unfortunately nothing came out, because frankly, I didn't have a rebuttal. She creamed me on that one.

After that I was more careful about opening my mouth, but I did keep my eyes peeled. At one point I put some hope in a mechanical quandary. One evening I commented, "Car's not starting right."

When Kim said something about calling our mechanic, I replied, "Probably just the starter motor. I can replace it myself and save us a lot of money."

"I really think we should call the mechanic," she said, but I finally convinced her there was no reason to waste money on something I could handle. After replacing the starter the very next morning, I began composing my speech about how Kim was obviously wrong about needing a mechanic, thus proving that women weren't always right after all. And it would have been a great speech too, if not for one little glitch.

The car wouldn't start.

"I'll call our mechanic," Kim sighed. "*And* a tow truck."

Turned out to be a loose wire. "No charge," our mechanic said. "But I should tell you that it looks like some con artist replaced your starter motor unnecessarily."

After the car incident my hope to debunk the "Women are always right" theory seemed to fizzle. But finally I realized something. It wasn't that Kim knew all the answers, it was simply that she didn't make a habit of claiming she did. She didn't go around making bold declarations on subjects she didn't know anything about. Interesting concept.

With that I said to Kim, "I know why you're always right."

She replied, "What?"

"You're always right because you don't have to be right."

"What in the world are you talking about?"

"If a car breaks down by the side of the road, what does a man usually do? A man gets out of the car and pokes around under the hood, even if he has the mechanical aptitude of cheese. A woman would never do that, because she's willing to admit it if she doesn't know anything about engines."

"It's a sweet thought," Kim said with a grin. "But the truth is a woman would never do that because she wouldn't want to mess up her nails. Or pass up a chance to talk on the cell phone. Why all this interest lately in who's right?"

I told her about my conversation with Skip and his claim that women are always right.

"Skip is messing with your head again. Obviously nobody is always right. You taught me that."

"Thanks a lot," I said.

"No, I mean that you're the one who's always saying never to assume anything. Never jump to conclusions before you know the whole story. Never claim to be right if you have no idea what you're talking about."

"I say that?"

Kim smiled at me and nodded.

"I guess," I said, "I should listen to myself talk more often…"

In today's battle about who's right, I think, it would also be good for men and women to listen to themselves *before* they talk. While there are many lighthearted observations and amusing generalizations floating around about gender differences these days, there can also be hurtful divisions when people become more concerned about being right than being in right relationship.

And in relationships, the less one needs to be right, the greater the chance that everything will turn out all right.

This Sporting Wife

When I mentioned earlier that women are smart to avoid sports, I didn't mean entirely. My wife and I enjoy various sporting events and activities together. We try to play tennis regularly and watch or attend the occasional game featuring our local NBA team, the Portland Trail Blazers. In the past we've even participated in church softball leagues.

I recall the summer we played on separate men's and women's teams. One evening I came home after a typically hard-fought contest featuring blazing line drives, hard slides into second base and intense glaring at the competition. "One of our guys," I told Kim, "even started a big argument with the umpire and got thrown out of the game."

"But we won!" I added triumphantly. "How about your game? Who won?"

After thinking a moment, Kim replied, "I don't exactly remember, but I saw my old friend Jane on the other team. It was great to catch up on what's been happening."

At that, I could only shake my head and smile. Wistfully, I mean. It struck me again that most women understand the spirit of church league softball far better than most men. As if winning really mattered more than simple fun and fellowship.

I don't mean to disparage healthy athletic competition. The Apostle Paul affirmed the spirit of athletics, after all, when he likened the journey of faith to a race: "Run in such a way as to get the prize. Everyone who competes in the games goes into strict training. They do it to get a crown that will not last; but we do it to get a crown that will last forever" (1 Cor. 9:24-25).

Of course, the goal of such a race isn't for one person to win, but for everyone to finish. And that's where modern sports (and sports fans) often become unhealthy—in the belief that winning is the only thing that matters.

A few years ago Kim reminded me about that again in another setting, though she wasn't necessarily trying to at the time. It happened when someone gave us tickets to a Trail Blazer game, and we gladly tooled off to Portland to attend the contest...

Our evening at the Blazer game started off like many other professional sports events I've attended over the years. As we settled into our seats, the hard-core fans were already going at it, shouting things like "Foul!" and "Get the ball!" and "Hey ref, are you *blind?*" And that was just during the team introductions.

Now, I'm not as big a sports fan as some, but I do follow basketball. So as the game got underway, I started getting into it. Throughout a tense first quarter I cheered and booed along with the rest of the fans as the lead changed hands several times. You can imagine my reaction, then, when Kim leaned over during a time-out and said, in a quote that may forever be etched in my mind, "That other team has pretty uniform colors."

I think it must have paralyzed me for a moment. It seemed like I sat there, slack-jawed, for a long time before I finally had to laugh. "The Blazers are behind by five," I said, "and you're rating the other team's uniforms?"

Kim gave a surprised expression and said, "The Blazers are behind?"

It was almost too much to take. I realized Kim was only a casual sports fan, but frankly wondered if that level of inattention was legal inside an NBA arena.

But as the contest raged on, I found myself being pulled back in. Even Kim, to my relief, seemed to get into the spirit. After a questionable call in the second quarter that put the other team on the foul line, she grabbed my arm and said with furrowed brow, "Can you believe it?"

"I know what you mean," I replied.

"So you think," she said, "that *is* the Governor and First Lady down there at courtside?"

With another look of exasperation, I inquired, "Aren't you even going to watch the game?"

"I am watching the game," Kim answered. "And everything else, too. Speaking of which, remember that cute apparel shop we passed on Level 2? I'm going to go check it out."

"But it's not even half time yet!" I protested.

"Exactly. Won't be crowded."

By then the game was beginning to lose its intrigue. How could I enjoy it if my wife, my partner, my pal, wasn't the least bit interested? Worse, what if she was out there laughing at me for caring about a dumb basketball game...?

That's when she suddenly appeared, loaded down with merchandise. But before I could express my dire disappointment that she'd doubly disgraced the game both by not caring and by using it as an excuse for shopping, I noticed what she bought: popcorn, nachos, colas and candy. It nearly brought tears to my eyes. "You do care after all," I admitted.

"Of course," she said. "Now who's playing again?"

I think she was kidding. At any rate, the game stayed close and exciting throughout the second half, and even Kim, to my great pleasure, showed signs of true fan spirit by booing the refs a few times. But it all got ruined at the end, I'm sorry to say, when the Blazers missed an easy shot and lost. Amid the groaning and weeping of the fans, Kim exclaimed perkily, "Wow! That was a great game!" I had to get her out of there quick, so we wouldn't get pelted with popcorn and warm sodas.

As we walked out into the night, all was gloom. Kim squeezed my hand and said, "What's the matter?"

"What's the matter? You saw it. They blew the game."

"Well, yeah," Kim said. "But that was only for 10 seconds. The rest of the game was pretty good, wasn't it?"

"Yeah, but…"

"Didn't you have fun?"

"Yeah, but…"

"Isn't this fun now?" Kim slipped her arm around me and I suddenly noticed what a pretty evening it was. The air was crisp, the city lights were sparkling, and the fountains in the arena square were splashing cheerfully.

"I guess it is," I admitted. And that's when I fully realized the beauty of not caring that much about sports. You could go to a game and enjoy it no matter what the outcome. What a concept. Sure it's nice when your team wins, but it's not as if it actually makes a difference in life, other than that considerably lighter feeling, after attending a game, in the general area of your wallet.

"You know," I said, reflecting on the evening, walking arm-in-arm through the frosty air with my partner and pal. "I have to admit that the other team's uniforms *were* pretty nice."

Signs for the Times

I 've been thinking about putting a sign in my wife's car that says, "No Gum Zone." Kim has a strange way with the stuff, if you ask me. She stretches one stick of gum by tearing it into four or five tiny pieces. And while I admire her thriftiness, little gum strips tend to escape and, well, gum up the works. Especially vulnerable is the dashboard area of her car, which at times can feature sun-scorched gum pieces fused to the plastic, or gooey gum wads lurking inside the glove compartment waiting to ambush the unassuming hand I stick in there. Hence the need for the "No Gum" sign.

Of course, Kim would probably like to put a "No Dribbling" sign above the bathroom sink. For unexplained reasons, I can never seem to keep water entirely where it belongs when I use the faucet. Somehow I manage to drip all over the fixtures, spray the mirror, and worst of all, dribble on the floor mat for Kim to come in wearing socks and *surprise*, get that annoying wet feeling on the soles of her feet.

But then I'd counter with a "No Opinions" sign in the bedroom. When dressing, Kim often asks, "How does this look?" To which I invariably answer, "Great!" I don't say that to cop out—she always looks great to me. But of course she never believes me and winds up going through five or six outfits, digging harder for my "honest" opinion ("Great!") with each one.

In reaction to my "No Opinions" sign in the bedroom, though, Kim might put up a "No Ignoring" sign on the fruit bowl in the kitchen. Kim works hard to keep fresh, healthful fruit in our daily diet, which is no easy feat living with a spouse whose favorite fruit is fresh-squeezed coffee beans. Left to my own devices, the fruit bowl is little more than decoration. Thinking about it, in fact, I wonder if the sign Kim would really like to put on the fruit bowl is "Eat This, Or Else!"

There are plenty of other signs we could probably think of—Kim could put a "No Leaving" placard on the leftovers, I might place a "No Sleeping" sign on the sofa for when we sit down at night to talk, and so on. But the whole thing would undoubtedly get out of hand. And the truth is, though signs like these might reflect some of the bothersome things that come up from time to time between spouses, the matters involved aren't all that serious.

Yet it's amazing how little things can become big issues in a marriage. It's astonishing how much ink and talk show time is given to serious marital problems such as fighting for the TV remote and whether the toilet lid stays up or down.

Since my wife and I are as prone as anyone to center on petty irritations, I've been thinking that the signs we really need in our house have nothing to do with gum or fruit, but with more pressing matters we can ignore without even realizing it. Here are a few signs that would probably be helpful to have around:

• **No Lording.** Before his wedding, an acquaintance of mine told a group of us married guys that his wife-to-be had no problem with the "honor and obey" part of traditional wedding vows. We looked at him incredulously and said, "She must really be old-fashioned."

"Yes," the acquaintance replied. "She *assumes* I'll obey her."

He was joking (I think), but somehow the quip made me sad. It reminded me that so many marriages today—so many aspects of gender relationships today—seem to center on who's in control. Who wins.

In such cases, we've already lost. "Submit to one another out of reverence for Christ," the Bible says about marriage (Eph. 5:21). The real issue isn't who will win, but who will serve. "No Lording" would remind us of that.

• **No Tracking.** Occasionally my wife and I will have a conversation that goes something like this:

Kim: "Did you forget to mail those bills like I asked?"

Me: "Maybe I did, but five years ago *you* forgot to record that check in the checkbook register!"

Whether it's me or her dredging up some long-ago mistake, it's usually just a sneaky diversion to avoid giving the right answer: "Whoops! Sorry!"

People talk about "hard sayings" in the Bible, but you can have the "Love your enemies" and "Sell all your possessions," tough as they may be. Because for me the hardest thing in the Bible is, "Love keeps no record of when it has been wronged" (1 Cor. 13:5 NLT). No referring to that forgotten check from years ago. No nursing that insensitive remark from weeks ago. No tracking daily mess-ups for future argument ammo. It's amazing how often spouses will use a loaded memory to blow each other out of the water.

• **No Jumping.** Another kind of conversation that has been known to go on in our house is:

Me: "I just wanted you to know that I think your idea about painting the inside of the garage is_"

Kim: "Yeah, I know, I know. Too dumb, too complicated, too expensive, too time-consuming, too everything, because it *is* just a garage and who needs to paint a garage even though it wouldn't look so dark and grungy and uninviting in there. But I'm just a girl, so what do I know about what to paint and what not to paint, right? Isn't that what Mr. Home-Improvement-Expert was going to say?"

Me: "Um, actually I was going to say your idea about painting the garage is great and we should get right on it."

Kim: "Oh! Ha ha! Right!"

The point is, we jump to conclusions at times. Marriage can be a hotbed for assumptions. Don't we always know what the other will say? Well, not really. That's why "No Jumping" signs are in order: "Be quick to listen, slow to speak, and slow to become angry" (James 1:19).

• **No Ripping.** It has often been said that one should never tear down his or her spouse in public. But obviously a lot of people have no qualms about it in private. It's sad to see so many spouses walking around all black and blue—not physically but emotionally and spiritually.

"Encourage each other and build each other up" (1 Thess. 5:11). Why is this so hard to do? Maybe we think that praising the other will somehow diminish ourselves. But when we lift them up, we too are raised. When we rip them apart, we too will bleed.

• **No Bobbing.** Modern life makes it ever easier to bob on the surface of marriage without getting deeper. We run from dawn until dark. We manage several careers. We shuttle the kids to nine activities a week. We keep computers and cell phones and pagers and faxes beeping all around us to make life more "convenient." We write "hug spouse" into our day books. In some ways marriage today looks more like running a small business than pursuing a big relationship.

We need the "No Bobbing" signs to remind us to quit skimming the surface of our relationships and take time to dive in. "Above all, love each other deeply, because love covers over a multitude of sins" (1 Pet. 4:8).

Now if you'll excuse me, I'm going to go cover over the pulverized gum on the dashboard that keeps getting on my nerves.

PART TWO

Sisters and Brothers

Your Church or Mine ?

Which Way to the Men's Service?

E arlier I mentioned my impression that many of to-day's women and men seek to get closer to one another by getting farther away from each other. Various relationship books and seminars are gender-tailored, so a man or woman can completely understand what makes a spouse or suitor or colleague tick long before setting foot in their general vicinity. Gathering a healthy set of expectations and assumptions about someone ahead of time, apparently, can spare the hassle of actually getting to know them personally.

I've already shared some of my concerns about that. Fortunately though, there is still a place where personal relationships are first priority. In this place women and men can look forward to meaningful fellowship and camaraderie and relational growth—by getting away from each other even more.

I'm referring to the church, of course, which continues to create bold new ways to break itself down into increasingly specialized people-groups. Or so it seems. Surveying the spiritual scene these days can be a little like channel-surfing on TV. One can find stations, er, services that are style-specific, age-specific, content-specific, taste-specific, program-specific, race-specific, income-level-specific and lots of other specifics.

Given such trends, can weekly gender-specific services be far behind? That might seem like a strange idea to some, but I'm not sure it's so far-fetched. During the gender-rally boom of the past few years, men and women have sometimes seemed more motivated to attend the latest *Promise Keepers* or *Women of Faith* event than their own local church. It would amaze me to hear the story of a guy so intent on making the big men's rally, for instance, he would travel hundreds of miles, sit in several hours of heavy traffic, sleep on a hard gym floor and squeeze through massive grid-locked crowds for the privilege of sitting all day in the nosebleed section of some sun-scorched stadium. A month later you might comment to the same guy, "Missed you at church last week."

"Yeah," comes the answer. "I had a sniffle."

So maybe gender-targeted rallies are on to something, given the enthusiasm they inspire. If we were to consider holding weekly male- or female-only services, what would they look like? Here are a few possible suggestions and benefits based on current gender stereotypes, er, I mean generalizations gathered from recent surveys and studies:

During the men's service…
- Less talking.
- There would also be less singing—maybe two songs, one being *How Great Thou Art* and another being to the tune of *Take Me Out to the Ball Game.*
- The sanctioned "Meeting and Greeting" exchange would be: Male 1: "How ya' doing?" Male 2: "Fine."
- Husbands could learn how to treat their wives without all those pesky interruptions from wives chiming in about what *they* want.
- All sermon illustrations would be about sports. In other words, not much different than now.
- Snacks and sodas would be available from pew vendors.
- Ceiling monitors could be installed when playoffs are on during service.
- Jesus' mushy command to "love one another" could be changed to "like one another pretty well."
- The official Bible translation would be RDCV—Readers Digest Condensed Version.

During the women's service…
- More talking.
- There would also be more singing with regular step-

aerobics segments, unless the church is already charismatic.

- Sale flyers would be added to the bulletin.
- Sermons could have more romantic content.
- Wives could review their husbands' faults without putting up with husbands' protests. In other words, not much different than now.
- Regular updates would be given on who's pregnant and/or who's changed hairstyles.
- Jesus' command to "Not worry about what you will wear" would be suspended on Sunday mornings.
- "Chocolate" could be seriously considered for a new communion element.
- The official Bible translation would be SPNV—Six-Part Novelized Version

I suppose gender separation in the church would never get this extreme, though, because some of us would actually prefer more integration rather than less. Many is the time I sit spouseless in the pew, wishing my wife could join me (or vice versa) more than once a month or so. But we're both so involved in various specialized ministries at our church, we rarely seem to cross paths any more.

Maybe it's just the wave of the future. One popular speaker has seriously suggested that the church retire its one-service-at-a-time tradition in favor of offering a half-dozen format options as churchgoers walk in the door at 10 AM Sunday morning. Beyond the usual groupings by age, style and demographics, I can only imagine some other kinds of specialized worship opportunities that might be offered:

• **Fashion-Specific Services.** Given the variety of clothing types seen at most church gatherings today—from suits to jeans—I had assumed that spiritual dress codes had disappeared long ago. Apparently not entirely. Only a couple of years back I was surprised to hear two separate judgments pronounced in relatively short succession. One person complained that a certain man displayed an obvious lack of maturity and commitment by engaging in the sin of...wearing an earring. Not long after, someone else expressed concern for another's lack of faith and compassion evident in the fact that he...wore a tie.

Perhaps these folks would have benefited from a multi-option format: Suits and dresses in one service, jeans and shorts in another, tattoos and body piercings in a third and so on.

• **Feeling-Specific Services.**   I've noticed that many worship CDs and tapes are produced these days with "mood themes," whether celebrative, reflective, inspiring, calming or others. The multi-option church could also tap into this. There might be services identified as Joyful, Thoughtful, Humorous, Dramatic and so on, so people could tailor their worship experiences to what they feel like hearing Sunday morning.

The only problem would be with the few who are less concerned about what they want than what they need. As my pastor-father once observed: "It's nice to hear people say, 'I enjoyed the sermon this morning.' But even better is when they tell you, 'I didn't enjoy the sermon very much, but I needed to hear it.'"

• **Climate-Specific Services.**   For several years when I served in my church as custodian, I would routinely receive feedback about the sanctuary being too warm or too cold. Sometimes it was both too warm and too cold on the same Sunday. It makes me think, given the variance in people's internal thermostats, that maybe the multi-option church would also offer Warm and Cool services.

Then again, perhaps this merely gets back to the idea of gender-specific services, given the notorious tendency of men and women to battle over temperature settings.

• **Technology-Specific Services.** With technology advancing so rapidly these days, churches have various choices about what kinds of high-tech equipment to integrate into worship settings. I remember three services I've attended in recent years that took different approaches to that. One reminded me of Star Trek, with flickering video monitors and blinking sound devices all over the stage. Another took a clean and streamlined approach—nary a music nor mic stand to be seen—to match its new, modernist surroundings. A third service incorporated no technology at all. Only an old wood podium and ancient upright piano graced the rustic meeting hall's stage area.

All these services were well-done and worshipful, but it surprises me to look back and pronounce the no-tech service as most meaningful to me. Maybe because it was different than today's norm. In that spirit, our multi-option church could offer the choice between a high-tech service, a medium-tech service, and a no-tech service.

• **Internet-Specific Service.** Now you may think I'm going too far, suggesting that people might "log on" for church rather than going to the trouble of attending personally. But it's probably already happening. It has also been speculated that churches of the future may well supply pew monitors and headphones so each churchgoer will be able to worship individually according to his or her preferred style and taste.

Frankly, the image scares me. Yet it may already be an apt metaphor for the state of modern church relationships: Sitting right next to each other, but miles apart.

Rally Ho!

L et me admit right off that I've never been much of a rally guy. I'm sure that's partly due to my introverted nature. I don't really like crowds. It's been said that introverts find refreshment in being alone, and eventually tire of spending time with others. Extroverts, by contrast, get energy from being with others, and don't enjoy spending too much time alone.

The line between introverts and extroverts isn't perfectly precise, of course, but my wife and I are a pretty good case study of the general principle. Kim likes to get out with a group, while I prefer to stay in with a book. Which is probably why we've had different reactions to the recent rally craze. Kim has enjoyed attending several women's rallies, while I've tended to avoid the men's events.

That hasn't been as easy as it sounds. For awhile the unspoken assumption in my area seemed to be that any truly committed Christian man would be a rally guy. As I think back to the height of the rally boom, I can hypothesize a series of events involving my imaginary liberal friend Skip T. Cull...

When the guys urged me to invite Skip to the big men's rally, I wondered if it would be a good idea. Rallies didn't seem like his thing. They seemed more like something Skip, as a liberal college professor, would criticize rather than embrace. But the guys kept after me to invite him. "Aren't you worried about Skip's soul?" someone asked.

"He already attends the Neighborhood church," I reminded.

"Our point exactly. You don't want him ending up in the fiery place where people go who are among the...you know, the D-word."

"You mean ..." I hesitated.

"Right. Democrats."

So I said I'd invite him. And when I did, I must admit that considering how long we'd known each other, I felt some shock and dismay at his response.

"Sure," he said. "I'd love to go."

How could he do that to me?

It's not that I don't enjoy Skip's company, but sometimes he makes me squirm. He has this annoying habit, for instance, of actually telling people how he feels. Once when some conservative friends of mine asked him what he thought about popular radio commentator Quick Crumlaw, Skip smirked and said, "Not too bad, I suppose, if you're partial to shoddy reporting, fudging of facts and vicious personal attacks masquerading as humor."

While my friends stood there in slack-jawed shock, I whisked Skip away from the threat of imminent injury and scolded, "Why on earth did you tell them what you really thought?"

Skip gave a puzzled look and said, "Didn't they ask?"

Sometimes you just can't reason with the guy.

And that's what worried me about Skip going to the big men's rally. What would he do there? Make 60,000 guys mad? I shuddered to think.

So I decided a little coaching session might be in order. I invited Skip over and sat him down. "What's your impression of these men's rallies?" I asked. "Do you know what they're all about?"

"Well," Skip replied, scratching his chin, "word around the college is that they stick voodoo pins in godless liberal dolls and plan how to recapture society from the evil feminists."

I stared at him, utterly speechless.

"I'm kidding!" Skip said with a grin. "You conservatives take everything so seriously. Actually, a colleague who attended one of these things told me it was all right. I'm glad you asked me to go. I've been wanting to see for myself."

I had secretly been hoping that Skip might decide to back out of the rally at the last minute, but so much for that. "OK," I said, "maybe I should just prepare you for a few things before we go so you know what to expect. You know, like the time just before I met that liberal polititian friend of yours when you reassured me that he didn't have horns and a pitchfork."

Skip nodded and I continued, "Now, how would you respond to a group of guys who spontaneously started shouting at you, '*We love Jesus, yes we do! We love Jesus...*'"

I motioned to Skip to finish the rhyme, upon which he straightened and rejoined, "*Good for you!*"

I shook my head and corrected, "*How 'bout you?*"

"Why would I say that?" Skip responded. "Wouldn't the fact that they already said 'We love Jesus' make it unnecessary for you to ask, 'How about you?'"

That was exactly why Skip drove some Christians crazy. Like there always had to be a reason for the stuff they did. Rather than attempting to argue the point of not having a point, however, I decided to move on to the next question.

"What if someone approached you with a T-shirt that read, 'WWJD?' I'm guessing you know what that stands for."

Skip thought for a moment and replied, "Which Way to the John, Dude?"

As I hung my head and breathed a deep sigh, Skip said, "I'm just pulling your leg again. Of course I know it means 'What Would Jesus Do?' A good question, especially when people really mean it rather than only pretending to care about what Jesus would do by wearing trendy WWJD shirts and wrist bands."

"Good point," I said, while making a mental note to avoid wearing my own WWJD shirt to the rally like I'd planned. "Now," I continued, "let's practice an important spiritual exercise we always perform at these events." I stood up and raised my hands, then immediately lowered my hands and sat down. Skip looked at me blankly.

"It's The Wave," I explained, which caused Skip to start snickering.

When I asked what he found so amusing, Skip replied, "I was just thinking of the great gathering of the saints mentioned in Revelation 5. In the majesty of the moment, I can just imagine the elders saying, 'Let's all do The Wave...'"

Hey, it could happen. But once again I decided to leave it alone and press on. "When you come to the merchandise booths," was my next question, "what will you buy?" This was no small matter, I explained, given the wide selection of available shirts, hats, CDs, books and other crisply marketed paraphernalia. But Skip confounded me once again by declaring, "I wouldn't buy anything."

Wouldn't buy anything? Hmm, unusual concept...

"That actually raises an interesting question," Skip added. "What should the guys wearing WWJD shirts and wrist bands do when they get to the merchandise booths? Overturn the tables and drive out the money changers? That's what Jesus did to the merchandise peddlers in the Temple."

It was definitely time to call it a day.

Needless to say, our little coaching session didn't put me much at ease the morning I picked up Skip and we headed for the rally. He seemed cheerful and relaxed the whole way there, which was more than I could say for myself. What would he spring on me next?

After we parked and strolled toward the stadium past the obligatory line of feminist protesters, Skip suddenly veered off and gave one of the assembled women—I still cringe to think about it—a hug.

I think I must have temporarily taken leave of my senses. The next thing I remember is standing there shaking hands with the woman, hundreds of passing eyeballs scorching my back, while Skip introduced her as a colleague from the college.

"Are you attending the rally?" she asked. Skip nodded and explained how I had invited him.

"Excellent," she said. "I'm writing an article about it for a sociology journal. Can I interview you two later? How about Monday lunch?"

Skip said we'd be delighted, and she disappeared among the protesters before I could graciously decline with words to the effect of, "Are you out of your mind?"

Thankfully, the rest of the day passed without incident. Skip didn't have much to say during the rally and seemed to take the whole thing in with that philosophical air of his. When we'd sat in traffic for awhile after the whole thing was over, he finally commented, "Aren't you going to ask me what I thought?"

"Do I have to?" I replied.

With a chuckle, Skip said, "Don't worry, for the most part I liked it."

"You did?" I asked in surprise.

"What's not to like about devotion to God and family, developing deeper relationships, ministering to others and living with integrity? Here's the thing that puzzles me though. Don't we already talk about those things every week at church?"

"I suppose," I replied, "though I can't say I always listen that carefully."

At that moment Skip raised an index finger and said "Aha!" in a way that could inspire only one response. Shut up and drive...

Skip looked around at all the exiting traffic and added, "That's what concerns me about these big Christian rallies that seem to be the thing nowadays. I hope people aren't thinking that a big spiritual push once in a while can replace the little spiritual steps a person has to take every day."

I looked at Skip and felt a wave of respect. Much of the time he was pretty philosophical, but once in a while he was just plain smart.

Tomorrow Today
Will Be Yesterday

A nother question I have about the rally trend is whether it inadvertently feeds off of discontent. My wife and I once attended a couple's event called "Bring Back the Joy." It was a good rally, but what was the theme really saying? That we couldn't possibly be happy with the current state of our marriage, and needed to restore some of its original luster? I doubt the rally intentionally meant to relay that message, but such a theme would be very much in line with the modern spirit. These days people don't seem very interested in living for today. All a lot of folks want to talk about is tomorrow or yesterday.

In so many areas of life people get hung up on how they think things *should* be, or the way they remember things *used* to be. "If only we could change this or that," they say, "everything would be great." Or, "If only we could go back to then or there, then we'd have it made." It goes beyond personal issues into social and political realms. Public debate and political campaigning in recent years have been dominated by the themes of "Preparing for the Promise (or Terror) of the Future" and "Returning to the Values (or Repressions) of the Past." I'm beginning to wonder if there's anyone left who just wants to be present.

Everywhere we go these days, neither the past nor the future will leave us alone. Say my wife and I head to the mall to buy some standard-issue blue jeans. I would likely find myself stuck with a choice between nostalgic slim-fitting Levi's that refused to travel further than my knees, and fashion-forward baggy blues that could comfortably house my entire family on a weekend camp-out. Kim, meanwhile, would face the horrors of retro 1970s hip-hugger bell-bottoms (much like a deer stunned by oncoming headlights) and next season's designer jeans with the price tag of last season's designer furniture.

So we bag the idea of finding acceptable jeans and decide to look for some comfortable shorts. But quickly we realize, after only an hour of wandering around various clothing stores, that this is July. At the height of shorts season, department stores look to the future by selling winter clothes, of course. Except for the occasional clearance rack of orange paisley or purple plaid shorts that were inexplicably in style last season.

Kim and I give up on clothes and stroll to the bookstore. There we're greeted by the Self Help shelf with its 100 variations of *Discovering the New You* (because you're surely not happy with your present flabby, boring, not making nearly enough money self) or *Recovering the Old You* (because everyone needs to release their Inner Child through strategic irresponsibility and blaming everything on everyone else). We aren't sure we want to discover any new selves, though, since our current selves already keep us pretty busy. And certainly we have no intention of releasing any inner children, given that our two actual children already wear us out enough.

So we clear out of the mall and drive to the home improvement center to buy a replacement faucet for the bathroom sink. All we can seem to locate, however, are historic-type fixtures for those new old-style homes builders are fond of constructing these days, and "next generation" hardware that is entirely incompatible with our current plumbing unless we replace the entire left side of our house.

That inspires us to take a break to think things over at the local coffee house. There we discover that they no longer serve plain old coffee and tea. "Not trendy enough," the clerk explains, urging us to try their hip new beverage called "Chai FrappicinoBerry Hot Iced

Skinny Herbal Mocha Soy Aromatherapeutic Latte." After explaining that we won't order anything that takes longer to say than to drink, we head next door to the 50s-style diner to get some good old-fashioned black coffee. Those were the days, we reminisce, when people started their day with a cup of strong motor oil seasoned with a crunchy spoonful of sand.

We decide to go home and try to salvage what's left of today. Kim picks up a magazine to read, but soon lowers it and says, "We've got a problem."

I turn from the news, where they're highlighting yesterday's tragedies and tomorrow's weather, and reply, "A problem? Excellent! Finally something to deal with *now.* What is it?"

"According to this article," Kim says, "Madisen doesn't have enough money for college."

"College?" I respond in disbelief. "But she's only four."

"Exactly. This chart says we should already have $67,500 saved up for her by now."

Getting weary of all this preoccupation with future and past, I try to pass off the whole matter by saying, "Maybe we can save extra money by eating out less."

"Which reminds me," Kim replies. "How come we never go out on dates anymore like we used to?"

The whole rest of the week continues like that. Everything is about yesterday or tomorrow. We have to catch up on things from last week, and fit things into the calendar for next week. We have to pay for things we charged last month, and charge things we have to pay for next month. We have to dig out plants that expired last season, and put in bulbs that won't come up until next season. We have to organize photos from last year's vacation, and make reservations for next year's vacation. And so it goes until Sunday morning, when I say to Kim with a sigh of relief, "Finally our day of rest. Now maybe we can just enjoy today for a change."

Silly me.

As soon as we walk into church, the worship leader launches into several choruses so new we don't know them, and several hymns so old we don't understand them. Next someone announces all the events that are coming up next week, and all the activities we still have to follow-up on from last week. Then comes news that there are seven new books in the library: four historical novels and three variations of "Getting Ready for the New Millennium."

A guest speaker follows who admonishes us to redeem the future by reclaiming the past. Society has abandoned its Christian heritage, the speaker says, and needs to recover the morals of the Bible and the 1950s, not necessarily in that order. Finally the pastor preaches about getting past the past by preparing for the future. We can't rest on our laurels, he says, but must always seek new and creative ways to minister. Which he could learn more about, incidentally, if the church would send him to the big "Getting Ready for the New Millennium" rally in Hawaii.

On the way home from church, Kim asks, "What did you think of the service?"

"I'm not sure I can tell you," I reply, "because today it's only acceptable to talk about yesterday or tomorrow. So I guess that means I could tell you tomorrow, because tomorrow today will be yesterday. You know what I mean?"

"Not a clue," Kim says as we pull into our driveway.

"I know what you mean," I respond, making my way wearily into the house. Apparently neither the past nor the future are planning on giving us any rest.

While I'm pondering this, however, our sofa comes into view and beckons me to stretch out and get comfy. And for the first time all week, I can say with no hesitation whatsoever: "There's no time like the present."

Witnessing Made Sleazy

My wife has this amazing ability to make a new friend, chat amiably about this and that, move beyond the surface to deeper personal issues and venture into the realm of faith and spirituality, all in the span of about 20 minutes. By contrast, it often takes me the better part of a month to get beyond "Hello" to something a little more meaningful, such as "What'd you say your name was again?"

Some would contend that's a guy thing, but I don't think it's necessarily the case. I know plenty of guys who have a natural talent for striking up meaningful conversations anywhere—at a ball game, on a park bench, during an entire five-hour flight to Atlanta. I think that's great, as long as I'm not the one sitting next to them on the plane to Atlanta.

But there's another type of Christian communication that does seem like a guy thing at times. I'm talking about gospel tracts. A few years ago while strolling along a downtown sidewalk, for instance, I happened to spy a trail of five-dollar bills strewn in the gutter. Picking some of them up, I discovered that they weren't real five-dollar bills, however. They were tracts. The front side was illustrated with the fake five-spots, and the back was printed with the ominous message:

DON'T BE FOOLED

The heart is deceitful above all things, and desperately wicked: Who can know it?
Jeremiah 17:9 (KJV)

Except a man be born again, he cannot see the kingdom of God.
John 3:3 (KJV)

On one hand, it was a fairly clever ploy. I did pick the tracts up, after all. On the other hand, though, I wasn't entirely charmed by the idea of litter as a Christian witness.

Perhaps I'm flirting with gender stereotypes here, but I don't think a woman would strew fake-money tracts in a gutter. I know my wife—who already has to admonish children and husband to pick up after themselves—couldn't do it. Nor would she attempt another tract tack I was party to recently. In the men's room of a restaurant, I noticed a little leaflet with a cover that shouted:

PORNOGRAPHY!

Suspecting it was a tract, I looked inside for sermonizing against lust, immorality and so on. What I found instead was intriguing:

The fact that you gave in to the temptation to look at this proves you are a hopeless sinner who needs to be saved. "For all have sinned and fall short of the glory of God" (Rom. 3:23). This means *you*, pervert!

OK, the tract didn't really contain that last sentence, but it may as well have, given the tenor of the thing.

As I said, I don't think most women would attempt to witness that way. And they would be right, of course. The practice of "friendship evangelism"—developing relationships with spiritually seeking people rather than aiming loaded tracts at them—has become the accepted norm.

But it wasn't always like that, at least in my experience. For some reason I have quite a few memories of being taught various witnessing "techniques." I remember once working through a manual (though I have no recollection of where or why) that outlined a number of "natural" dialogues and bodily poses aimed at making one's victim, er, prospect feel entirely at ease about the idea of getting saved.

One diagram sticks in my mind. The witnesser grips the witnessee's shoulder in one hand, and in the other holds

an open Bible the size of a sofa cushion (also for cream-
ing the prospect, perhaps, in case of an attempted escape). From that illustration, I can still imagine the well-
trained Christian being ready for any and all heathens
who may happen by: "Excuse me sir, but I want you to
know that God loves you, and, uh, wait a minute, it's here
in my manual somewhere... Fire and Brimstone, Going to
Hell, Last Judgment...oh, here it is, God loves you and *I*
love you too! Sir? Sir? Hey, where are you going?"

No one seeking to share his or her faith would really
be that tactless, I suppose. But then again maybe they
would. Not long ago at a freeway rest area, I came out
of the men's room and encountered a fellow giving out
books titled *Finally the Real Truth About Bible Prophecy*,
or something like that. Gathering upon closer examina-
tion that it was one of those alarmist-type tomes that
tend to contain some "stretchers" ("Bill Gates spelled
backwards while changing only two letters and cutting
out 'Bill' is 'Satan!'"), I handed the book back and polite-
ly explained, "Thanks for the offer, but I'm already a
church member."

"That doesn't mean you're a Christian," he said endearingly. Which could have been true, I suppose, but
since we'd never met before and he knew absolutely
nothing about me, the statement struck me as being a
tad presumptuous.

But alas, I've done the same thing. Back during the
mid-1970s Jesus Movement, the Southern California
youth group I attended was in the habit of going beach
witnessing every Saturday. We'd pair up and take tracts
or concert flyers to pass out, looking for chances to
share with people on a more personal level. I wasn't
very good at it. While others in our party seemed to
have the same knack as my wife for immediately engaging people in meaningful conversation, I'm sure I
often came across like the guy at the rest area who approached me with the prophecy book. When encoun-
tering someone, I was usually more concerned about

what I wanted to say than about listening to or trying to understand that person. It's a fault that has plagued Christian witnessers all too often over the centuries.

Tellingly, my most vivid recollections from that year-long beach witnessing period have nothing to do with things I said to people, but with a couple of instances in which there was nothing I *could* say. I should mention that the beach we frequented was well-known as a hangout for famous Southern Californian eccentrics and "free thinkers." One time when I asked an average-looking beachgoer if he'd be interested in attending a concert our church was sponsoring, he replied with utter sincerity, "I'm so sorry, but I'm already booked on tonight's flight to Neptune." As hard as I tried, I just couldn't think of a helpful comeback for that.

In another encounter, I greeted a passing fellow and realized with a start that he was wearing an "LA Lakers" T-shirt. Which might have been less surprising if it wasn't the *only* thing he was wearing. Again I was speechless. Later, I did think of a potentially helpful exchange in such a situation, however:

Passerby: "Might you have any suntan lotion? My shins are getting burned."

Me: "I don't have any lotion, but did you know that the Lord can cover a multitude of shins?"

And it's also a good thing that building relationships has taken priority over trying techniques when it comes to sharing one's faith. Which means that my wife, as I'd always suspected, has been right all along.

More power to her. She probably could even have struck up a meaningful conversation with the Neptune guy. "So tell me," I can hear her saying, "how many frequent flyer miles is that?"

Jump For Jesus

We ran into our old friend Fad Franklin at the gas station. After helping him back to his feet and making sure he wasn't hurt, I asked what he'd been up to lately.

"This and that," he said, strolling over to the back of his car and leaning conspicuously beside a bumper sticker that read, **Jump for Jesus.**

My wife and I looked at each other as if to say, "We don't want to go down that road." Fad was the kind of guy who got into something new every few months, whether it was pursuing a hot business opportunity, engaging in a new form of recreation, or launching some kind of, well, *interesting* ministry strategy. Last time we'd seen him he was working on something called **Bowling for Jesus**, but claimed he was being thwarted by religious persecution on league nights.

So we didn't really want to know what Jump for Jesus involved. Parachutes? Bungee cords? It had an ominous sound to it.

"How's Madge and the kids?" Kim asked, attempting to avoid the inevitable.

"Just fine," Fad replied, pulling a blue towelette from the station's dispenser and squatting down to polish the **Jump for Jesus** sticker. "Yep, they're really jazzed about my new ministry idea."

Fad wasn't making this easy. "How's work going?" I tried, figuring he couldn't resist going on about some recently hatched money-making venture. And sure enough, his eyes lit up and he exclaimed, "I've gotten into the bumper sticker business!"

Great.

"It's big," Fad continued. "We've produced several best sellers, like **WWJDRV?** (What Would Jesus Drive?) and **I'd Rather Be Right Than Left**. Get it? It's about politics *and* the rapture. And then there's our most popular sticker to date, the Christian fish eating the Darwin fish eating the Christian fish eating the Darwin fish eating the Christian fish eating the Darwin fish. At least I think that's the current number of fish. Oh, and this is my latest," Fad concluded, framing the **Jump For Jesus** sticker with his hands.

We knew we were licked. With a sigh I inquired, "So what does this Jump for Jesus mean, anyway? I didn't know you were charismatic."

"Oh, it's not about that," Fad said, straightening up. "It all came to me a few months ago when I got to thinking, what could we Christians do to really make a difference in this town? And I thought about all the other publicity stunts, er, I mean outreach opportunities that had been staged. Already there was March for Jesus, Run for Jesus, Hike for Jesus, Bike for Jesus, Hop On One Foot for Jesus, Sit for Jesus, Shop for Jesus, Dine for Jesus, Whine for Jesus, Sleep for Jesus, Skateboard for Jesus, Sailboard for Jesus, Snowboard for Jesus, Be Bored for Jesus, and probably a few I'm forgetting. And of course you know the kind of impact those events made."

Kim and I looked at each other blankly, then turned to Fad and said, "Of course."

"That's right," Fad nodded. "They made the local papers. So I got to thinking, what hasn't been done yet, what hasn't been done yet? And that's when it all came to me in a vision: Jump for Jesus. And the beauty of the idea was that it wouldn't involve plain old manual jumping or jumping on trampolines, which has been done to death, but a great jumping movement sweeping the entire downtown area. And do you know how?"

After another moment of silence during which it became clear that we hadn't the slightest idea how, Fad yelped triumphantly, "Pogo sticks!"

We did have to grant that was indeed quite a vision. And when Fad quipped, "We'll have the place jumpin'!" accompanied by his distinctive mega-decibel laugh, I'd

venture to say that the vision became very nearly nau-
seating.

But we were heartened somewhat when Fad began
to explain that the theme he envisioned for the Jump
for Jesus event would come from Acts 3:8, where Peter
and John healed the lame man. That captured the spirit of the thing, Fad said, the man who went "walking
and jumping, and praising God."

"Oh," Kim rejoined with heightened interest. "So
you're going to help needy people along the way, like
Peter and John did?"

Fad furrowed his brow and replied, "Well, no. That
would distract us from our bigger purpose."

"I think I get it," I offered. "You want to get past giving token help to the needy, and send a message to
the community that they should pay attention to the
needs of the helpless and hurting every day."

A knowing smile spread across Fad's face and he ac-
knowledged, "You're kidding, right? Surely you realize
we're angling for the biggest fish of all. The ultimate
ministry opportunity."

Once again we indicated that we were stumped.

"Making the Six O'clock News, of course!" Fad bel-
lowed. "I can see it all now—reporters, camera people,
news choppers..." With that Fad pulled a pogo stick
from his car and started bouncing around the gas station lot. In front of the auto repair bay he must have
hit a bump, though, because suddenly he shot sideways into the garage, only to emerge a moment later
apologizing profusely to the mechanic and removing a
tangle of fan belts from around his neck and arms.

"By the way," he said, striding back and continuing
the conversation as if nothing had happened, "I've
been wondering why I never see you guys at any of
these big ministry events. What gives?"

Lowering my voice and motioning for Fad to come
closer, I said, "I want to let you in on a little secret.
For awhile now we've been involved in developing the

absolute, ultimate ministry."

Fad gasped and said, "No. How come I haven't heard of it?"

"Well, it isn't a one-time event or a mass meeting targeting certain kinds of people, and it doesn't make the news because it mostly involves ordinary people doing ordinary things."

With a puzzled look, Fad asked, "Ordinary? Then how can it be the ultimate?"

"That's the thing. Somehow these ordinary people doing ordinary things are linked to a vast network of ministry that touches people of all ages, classes, cultures, needs and walks of life. And the exciting part is, it doesn't just happen once or twice a year, it goes on every week."

"Well," Fad urged, "what is it?"

I looked around dramatically, then motioned to Kim. She leaned in and whispered, "It's our church."

For a moment Fad just gave a blank stare. Then he suddenly let out a booming laugh and said, "Ha! You really had me going there for a minute. But it does get me thinking. Ultimate Ministry, Ultimate Ministry. Has a nice ring to it. What would you do on Ultimate Ministry Day? Lasers and smoke bombs? Supersonic air show? Celebrity worship contest? Hmm, this has possibilities…"

With that we discretely got Gassed Up for Jesus and drove away from the station while Fad continued his Ultimate Ministry monologue. I do admit to feeling a pang of concern, though. If Fad did manage to pull off Ultimate Ministry day, what would he do for an encore? What spiritual accomplishment would there be left?

He might even have to stoop to going back to church.

Telling It Like It Isn't

Several years ago I was asked to come up with a name for the young married's Sunday school class I was teaching at our church. After thinking for a moment, I suggested, "How about 'Young Married's Sunday School Class?'"

"Ha ha," my inquirer responded. "No, really. You need to come up with a name by the end of the month."

I wasn't joking about "Young Married's Sunday School Class." Alas, neither was the name solicitor, who apparently wanted something more catchy than accurate. So I came up with a list of possible titles:

CUSS (**Co**Uples **S**unday **S**chool)

"Hour A How'r Ya"

"Half An Hour A How'r Ya, By the Time Everyone Wanders In."

YAMMER (**Y**oung **A**dults **M**aking **M**inds of **E**xcellent **R**epute)

YAHOOZ (**Y**oung **A**dults **H**aving a sn**OOZ**e)

"Snappy Name Masquerading As Young Married's Sunday School Class."

I never shared the list, however, for fear that the name solicitor might accuse me of failing to take the naming project seriously. I don't know how he could get that idea. At any rate, I finally decided on the name "20/20s." When I submitted this to the name seeker, he essentially responded, "I have no idea what that means. It's perfect."

What I'd meant to infer with "20/20s" was our class's general age group (20 to 40) and specific goal (sharpening our spiritual vision through Bible study and discussion). Few would catch on to that without an explanation, of course. And that got me thinking about the power of a properly mischosen name. If you call something "Young Married's Sunday School Class," people will instinctively yawn and say, "Same old thing." If you call something "20/20s," by contrast, people will raise their eyebrows with interest and say, "Who thought up that weird name?"

That's what I still occasionally hear from newcomers to our class, anyway. But I just take it as a sign of our times. People don't want the same old stuff, so all kinds of snappy new names are given to the same old stuff. In order to jazz up a boring item like a "car," for example, an advertiser might refer to it as a "driving experience." Obviously it works. These days people trade in their dull, perfectly paid for old "cars" for overpriced, debt-loaded new "driving experiences" with alarming frequency.

Examples of this kind of hype appear everywhere. The release of an unmemorable new movie becomes a "motion picture event." A mundane sports contest is an "epic battle." A lame excuse to spend money on stuff nobody really needs is a "huge sale." Unimaginative network programming becomes "must see TV." The network that employs that phrase did even better at concept-twisting recently with a campaign to liven up the ho-hum image of "reruns": "If you haven't seen it, it's new to you!"

I've thought off and on about this term-bending phenomenon for a long time. It probably started back in high school, when I took a summer job in a large vegetable cannery. I worked the green bean season, during which seasonal employees were given the choice of a number of different assignments described by various job titles. The one that sounded most appealing and prestigious to me was "Sanitation Engineer." Granted, I wasn't very bright. I was entirely unaware at that time that "sanitation" referred to "garbage." So I spent the summer cleaning disgusting cannery muck off the machinery and shoveling decomposing bean plant remains out of what was affectionately known as the "goat shed" for its, shall we say, extremely aromatic atmosphere.

Good thing they'd renamed the job "Sanitation Engineer" from its original title describing the person who breathed goat shed fumes all summer: "Sanity Endangered." Otherwise nobody would have volunteered. Come to think of it, I was the only one who did.

A number of years later I came across an intriguing article that termed this kind of thing "doublespeak." Apparently the practice of camouflaging reality with flowery language was a rapidly growing trend. The article quoted a number of doublespeak examples pulled from actual reports published by various U.S. government agencies:

- **Safety related occurrence** (translation: accident)
- **Advanced downward adjustment** (budget cut)
- **Aerodynamic personnel decelerator** (parachute)
- **Facial olfactory characteristic** (nose)
- **Wood interdental stimulator** (toothpick)
- **Portable hand-held communications inscriber** (pencil)

I loved that last one. From then on I could imagine asking my wife every time the need came up, "Have you seen my portable hand-held communications inscriber anywhere?" To which I could fathom her responding after awhile in frustration: "If you don't start saying 'pencil' like a normal person, I'm going to stick a wood interdental stimulator up your facial olfactory characteristic."

It was the "young married's Sunday school class" incident that got me thinking about doublespeak in the church. Where there used to be plain old Sunday school classes, worship services and Bible studies, churches now offer amazing varieties of gatherings and events that can best be described as Sunday school classes, worship services and Bible studies. But now they all have catchy names, like "20/20s."

Yet even though I've been complaining about it, that

kind of naming is probably harmless for the most part. We want people to be intrigued by ministry activities rather than view them as potential yawners.

Where church-related doublespeak can become disturbing, however, is in the modern tendency to water down some of the gospel message. We like to share ideas such as love and acceptance, for example, but aren't always so clear anymore on subjects like commitment and loyalty. We love the idea of God blessing us, of course, but get a bit nervous about the call to serve others. We think forgiveness is fantastic, obviously, but would frankly prefer to get rid of sin.

Not the practice, I mean, but the concept. And we're doing a pretty good job of it. Sin is not one of the hottest topics going these days, unless of course it's someone else's. When it comes to our own sin, though, better to call it (as we've heard several politicians and TV preachers say in recent years) a "moral lapse" or "momentary failure."

In the spirit of the government-issued doublespeak I quoted earlier, I can even think of some easier-to-swallow terms for more specific sins...I mean moral lapses:

- **Enhanced self-worth** (translation: pride)
- **Consumer confidence** (greed)
- **Personality discernment** (judging)
- **Peace action** (war)
- **Constructive criticism** (destructive criticism)
- **Rift management** (divisiveness)
- **Fellowship** (gossip)
- **Para-marital social proximity** (infidelity)
- **Free speech** (obscenity, pornography, racism, sexism, hate, etc.)

These types of sin-softening terms wouldn't really be needed in our anything-goes age, however. There's already a popular doublespeak statement widely used for "sin": "It's somebody else's fault."

What's Your Style?

A number of us had gathered together from various North American churches for a multi-day study conference. On Sunday morning we took a break from our work to attend a local worship service. Since there were several churches in the area we could potentially visit, a discussion ensued about the particular personality and approach of each one. After deciding which church to attend and heading in that direction, we fell into discussion about our own congregations. "So," someone asked another, "what's your style?"

For some reason that struck me funny. It occurred to me at that moment how completely we've come to describe our modern church experience by worship style. Is it contemporary, traditional, blended, classical, charismatic, country or what? The thing that amused me about "What's your style?" was how closely it echoed the familiar singles-bar line, "What's your sign?" Upon reflection, however, I realized the similarities may have gone deeper. Is the recent epidemic of congregation-hopping and church-shopping really that different than cruising the singles scene, always looking for something or someone better?

As I consider the implications of "What's your style?", an interesting scenario fills my imagination...

One morning while my wife and I lounged at the counter of our local coffee house, a sharp-looking woman slid onto the next stool and smiled at me in a way that almost made me drop my mocha. As the woman attempted to engage me in conversation, I glanced over at Kim, who didn't seem bothered by it. The woman and I visited a bit, until the moment she disconcerted me by touching my arm and cooing, "Well then. What's your style?"

I knew I shouldn't have let it go any further than that. I was already in a committed relationship, after all. But before I could stop myself I replied, "Blended. You know, hymns and choruses, that sort of thing."

She shook her head and said, "Too bad. I would have figured you for a more contemporary kind of guy."

When Kim gave a snort on the other side of me, I protested, "I think I am a contemporary kind of guy."

"Then why have you settled for blended? You can do better than that. As they say, you gotta shop around."

"That seems to be the drift," I agreed, "but I don't know…"

"What's not to know?" she interrupted. "No harm in looking. Would you like to check out our 10 A.M. contemporary service this Sunday?"

I was about to say *no* when Kim interjected, "Maybe we should. We can still make our 11 A.M. service without missing more than a hymn or two. No great loss."

"That's the spirit," the woman encouraged, getting up to leave. "See you there."

"I'm not so sure about this," I told Kim. "I'll grant you that 11 A.M. isn't exactly trendy or cutting edge, but I think we owe it a *little* courtesy after all these years."

"Well, maybe it owes us a little courtesy too," Kim said. "We've given some of the best years of our lives to 11 A.M., but do we get back the happiness we deserve? They're always going on about depressing subjects like 'sin' and trying to get us to do stuff in the church. It gets tiring."

True enough. So I agreed to go to 10 A.M. As the woman said, no harm in looking.

I still had some misgivings, though, when we arrived Sunday morning. But not for long. The service was just fantastic. From our comfortable theater seats we enjoyed the most upbeat and entertaining music, drama and preaching you could possibly imagine. Best of all, there wasn't even one mention of the word "sin." How could we resist? We didn't even bother trying to make it to our regular 11 A.M. service.

After only a few months had passed, however, we started getting a little weary of 10 A.M. It was still endearingly entertaining and eminently professional, to be sure, but a little more air-headed than we'd noticed at first. The constant Top Ten lists, endless chorus repeats and interchangeable McSermons were getting to us. Granted, they did try to get us interested in more demanding weeknight Bible studies and small groups, but what kind of self-respecting church couldn't meet all our needs in an hour on Sunday morning?

While we were discussing that one morning at our local coffee house, a smart-looking man slid onto the next stool and gave a friendly hello. He opened a thick book and began reading. Now, I'm not the kind of person who usually bothers readers or bores people on airplanes, but in this case I was so starved for intellectual stimulation I just couldn't help myself. "What's that you're reading?" I asked.

He told me, and we fell into an interesting discussion about books, current events and a variety of other subjects. Somewhere along the line, during a pause in the conversation, he ventured, "If you don't mind my asking, what's your style?"

I looked at Kim, and she nodded. We told him the whole story of how we'd previously been blended, then moved to contemporary, but now were wondering if we were stuck in a trendy rut.

"I know what you mean," our companion mused. "Pardon me if this seems too forward, but would you be interested in visiting our 9 A.M. liturgical service this Sunday? You might find it engaging."

We said thanks for the offer, and that we'd think about it. After the man left, Kim said, "We have been attending 10 A.M. for only a few months, so maybe it wouldn't be polite to leave it for another service so soon."

"Who'd notice?" I asked. "It's never the same congregation twice over there. I think we should try 9 A.M."

So we did. And it was heavenly. The stained glass in the old stone sanctuary was glorious and the pipe organ breathed graceful strains of Bach. We were thoroughly enchanted. It was the polar opposite of 10 A.M. We sang great old wordy hymns and joined in thoughtful readings and prayers. The pastor addressed us in reasonable, well-researched tones rather than relying on jokes and sports anecdotes. Refreshing.

For awhile. After a few more months, though, we began to tire of Bach, written prayers and abstract sermons involving the concept of "Christ consciousness." I mean, it was all very tasteful and cerebral, but lacked a certain passion. Amazingly, we found ourselves longing for a bit of fire and brimstone.

While Kim and I contemplated this one morning at our local coffee house, a jaunty-looking fellow wearing cowboy boots and Wrangler jeans clopped in and hopped up on the next stool. "Howdy there," he exclaimed, clapping my shoulder. The guy was considerably older than me, but appeared to be a lot tougher and stronger than I would ever be. After spending so much time with intellectuals recently, I liked that. As we visited he seemed very friendly and down to earth.

After a bit he suddenly said, "So tell me there, pardner, what's your style?"

Once again we told our sad story about how we'd started out blended, then moved on to contemporary, and now more recently had been liturgical. "But lately," I said, "we've been finding it kind of, well, kind of…"

"Boring?" the cowboy finished. "Sounds like you need a good old-fashioned foot-stomping revival. Hows about coming to our 8 A.M. country gospel service Sunday? We'll git yer blood flowing again."

Needless to say, we went. Country gospel had never been our style, but there was something about it here that seemed unusually appealing and energetic. The music was pleasingly fast, the prayers engagingly loud, and the stomping and clapping and arm-waving healthfully aerobic. And when the preacher preached, God bless him, he sounded like he *meant* it, rather than droning on like it was some kind of theology seminar. Not only did we hear the word "sin" for the first time in months, we heard it 52 times. We rather enjoyed it.

For a few months, anyway. Eventually, though, the whole thing started giving us headaches. All that shouting and stomping and carrying on. Then finally one Sunday, it happened. We couldn't bring ourselves to get out of bed for the 8 A.M. country gospel service, and thought well, maybe we should just get up for our former 9 A.M. liturgical service. But 9 A.M. came and went, and we began to discuss giving the 10 A.M. contemporary service another chance. But we were still lying around listlessly at 10 A.M., looking at each other wondering, now what?

Then it dawned on us. If we felt that 10 A.M. was too trendy, 9 A.M. was too brainy, and 8 A.M. was too country, what kind of situation were we really looking for? Blended. So we jumped up, got dressed, and headed for the 11 A.M. service at our original church.

But when we arrived, something was odd. We kept expecting to see old friends and familiar faces, but didn't seem to recognize a single person. Not a soul. Then we finally realized, looking around and shrugging our shoulders at each other, what had happened. Everyone had left and gone to other churches, and people from other churches had left and come here. It was weird.

Finally the time had come to consider some critical questions. What were we to make of the strange style-shifting state of the modern church? How were we to feel about coming back to a familiar church filled with unfamiliar people? How could we describe the experience of knowing no one and being known by no one?

As the instruments started to play and we stood with these strangers to sing, we didn't quite know what to make of it. But at least the music was cool.

PART THREE

Mothers and Fathers

Parenting the Queazy Way

In The Beginning...

I know a guy who once gave a rather interesting response to the news that his wife was expecting their second child. "Great," he said, grabbing her hand supportively. "More bills!"

Needless to say, it wasn't exactly the response his wife was hoping for.

But face it, when it comes to the subject of childbirth, we men are still rank amateurs—and sometimes more rank than amateur. It's only in recent years, remember, that we've begun to accompany our wives to childbirth classes and into delivery rooms to "assist" in the birthing process. So we'll have to be excused, when we're told that a new little bundle is on the way, if we say brainless things like "Another one?" or "How did happen?"

Fortunately I didn't say something that dumb when my wife informed me of the impending arrival of our second. I said something dumber. Recalling the experience gained from our first, I encouragingly declared, "At least it will be easier this time." No doubt remembering the 15 hours of painful labor *and* the Cesarean section it took to deliver our oldest, Kim shot me a look that said, "Easy for you to say!"

Nothing really prepared me for the long, grueling experience of our first labor and delivery—though I do have to give the hospital credit for trying. They offered a seven-week childbirth class, which Kim and I dutifully attended. I must say that it put my vague fears about what to expect into much better perspective. Before the seven-week course I wasn't really sure what I was afraid of, but afterward I knew what I was afraid of. Here are some highlights from each week's session...

Week One: The major theme was "Nutrition." The instructor outlined the importance of maintaining a proper diet and participating in regular exercise. She must have noticed during all the talk about bran flakes and broccoli florets, however, that a few of us husbands were dozing off a little, possibly dreaming of deep-dish pizza and chocolate chip cookies. "A good diet," she emphasized, "is just as important for Daddy as it is for Mommy over the coming months."

We husbands snickered to ourselves and thought, "Yeah, right. What do our diets have to do with anything?"

The instructor merely smiled as if to say, "Trust me."

We should have. It wasn't long before I became quite familiar with the concept, "Sympathy Pregnancy." As my wife expanded around the middle, I seemed to develop an urgent desire to keep up by eating everything in sight.

Week Two: The subject was "Labor and Delivery," and the discussion seemed to center around two main themes:

1). After an hour of lecturing and diagrams, I gathered that how one tells that true labor has started is by the following method: time the contractions, nod thoughtfully, time the contractions again, and then take an entirely random guess. Most of the time you'll be wrong anyway, and will get sent back home from the hospital to guess again.

2). In order to warn, I mean inform us about what to expect, we watched an extremely true-to-life video called "The Miracle of Birth," or something like that. I think there may have been scenes during which some of the fathers actually looked away. But not me. You'd be surprised how much you can still see through the little cracks between your fingers.

In the parts I did see, the video reminded me that childbirth involved a lot of potentially unpleasant things like pain, screaming, heavy breathing, fainting, hyperventilating and so on. And apparently it wouldn't be so easy for Mommy, either.

Week Three: The theme was "Cesarean Delivery." The instructor said we had to cover this scary subject, just in case the situation came up for any of us in the class. I didn't really want to hear it. Only weeks earlier a friend of mine had responded to the news that Kim and I were expecting by pulling out explicit pictures of his own wife's recent Cesarean. As I attempted to avoid looking, he boasted. "I watched the whole thing."

My friend's courage caused me to reconsider my feelings about a possible Cesarean and conclude, "There is no way I could watch something like that and remain conscious." During the Cesarean session, then, it gave me hope to be reminded that a much smaller percentage of women had Cesarean deliveries rather than routine deliveries. So it wouldn't happen to us, right? Right? Hmm...

Week Four: We covered newborn care. I'd already had a few of the traditional nightmares involving this subject, such as the "bobbling the baby on the way down the stairs" dream and the "tripping over a toy and sending the baby flying" scenario. Newborns seemed so fragile. Could a clumsy old Daddy break one?

The instructor assured us that we would be all right with a bit of prudence and careful handling. My fears about that were soon overshadowed, anyway, by what I perceived to be a much greater threat to the safety and sanity of new parents: The Attack of the Baby Stuff.

I was utterly astounded at the vast array of implements needed for modern parenthood. Our instructor had them spread all over the stage of the lecture hall like a nursery showroom display. There were cribs, cradles, carriers, car seats, baby swings, changing tables, chew toys, learning toys, diaper bags, bottles, burp rags, baby wipes, blankets, pacifiers, breast pumps, stuffed bunnies, butterfly mobiles and other items I couldn't even identify.

That's when I realized the often-asked question, "Will a baby fit into our life?" was less philosophical than literal.

Week Five: The discussion was about whether to breast or bottle feed the new baby. Our instructor stated that she obviously couldn't determine the best course of action for each of our situations. But barring complications, she said, breast feeding was probably the preferable way to go.

I agreed. It seemed evident to me that the natural route would most effectively promote health, bonding, convenience, cost-effectiveness, and most importantly, Daddy's chances to sleep peacefully through those grueling middle-of-the-night feedings.

Or so I thought. When I said as much to Kim, she smiled slyly and said, "Apparently you weren't paying attention during last week's demonstration of the breast pump."

Gulp.

Week Six: The hot topic was the father's role in the delivery room. We discussed and diagrammed many details of being an effective labor and delivery "coach." From several pages of material, I condensed my task down to what I saw to be a few crucial details:

Don't faint.

Bark "breathe!" at random intervals.

Let Mommy hold my hand without me screeching while she tries to crush it into bone meal.

Quietly take abuse about this whole mess being Daddy's fault.

Be unfailingly cheerful and encouraging even when it all makes me want to curl up on the floor in the fetal position.

Under no circumstances make comments about the good old days when Daddies got to sit around in the waiting room reading magazines.

Don't rush out of the room in horror if the doctor suggests I cut the umbilical cord.

Never ask Mommy, "Does it hurt?"

Week Seven: When I learned that the last childbirth class would be about breathing methods, my initial thought was that it would be unnecessary to attend. Once we got to the hospital, I personally wasn't planning on breathing until our baby was safely delivered.

But it was really a session about breathing and relaxation techniques during labor, of course, to help make the scary and painful process more manageable. So I decided the breathing class would be helpful for managing labor after all—but how was Kim going to make it through?

The big event did arrive soon enough. We guessed right about labor, drove to the hospital and checked into the maternity ward. It was nothing like all the comical rushing around in movies and comedy shows, but rather seemed to take eons. Everything went in slow motion, where Kim had the distinct displeasure of experiencing the worst of both worlds. As I mentioned, not only did she attempt a routine delivery through 15 hours of labor, she finally had to have a Cesarean anyway. Despite the complications, everything turned out all right. Holding my new son in my arms, in fact, I had to say that everything turned out beautifully.

Still, when Kim gave me the news three years later that we'd be doing it all again, some of the scarier parts from the first time did come to mind. I think I can be forgiven for responding, "At least it will be easier this time." How could it not be?

So you can imagine our shock when we finally went in to deliver our second and . . . it all went like clockwork. After only a few hours, our daughter was born. Entirely routine. Kim and I kept looking at each other as if to say, "Something's wrong, everything's going right!" But we should have realized, I suppose, that sequels are generally less exciting than the first.

This time, it was quite all right with us.

Toys R Among Us

I mentioned that the arrival of a new baby into a modern couple's household tends to be accompanied by an astounding amount of stuff. But as the child outgrows his or her crib, cradle, carrier, car seat, baby swing, changing table and so on, everything changes. You collect even more stuff. By the time our oldest had hung around for only a couple of years, our home had gotten so full of stuff that my wife and I had to seriously consider moving into a tent in the back yard.

Well, maybe it wasn't quite that bad, but it was bad enough. The stuff situation was magnified for us by the double whammy of having both a small house and a large number of relatives in the area. You never knew when a family member would show up bearing the fruit of yet another Toys R Us harvest: "We just happened to see these 11 or 12 items on display and couldn't resist buying them for the little guy!"

So with our generous relatives delivering stuff and we ourselves buying even more stuff, our home became rather stuff-intensive. And while I'm sure we all meant well, some of the stuff entered the premises with mixed results…

• **Baby Bouncer.** This spring-loaded contraption was like a toddler bungee cord—you clamped it to the top of an open door frame and strapped Junior into the low-hanging seat below. That way his little legs could reach the ground so he could bounce and bounce and bounce until he either threw up, or the doorframe came crashing down on top of him. OK, I'm kidding about the doorframe, but I did worry about it!

That was another great thing, in fact, about all the newfangled toys and gizmos that came with modern parenthood—more things for Daddy to panic about.

• **Mini Car.** This was one of those orange plastic, surprisingly nimble vehicles shaped like the original Volkswagen Beetle, only bigger. Seth could climb in, get his feet pumping Flintstone-style, and proceed to knock large chunks of plaster off the living room walls. In good weather, fortunately, we could salvage some of the plaster by taking the car outside for him to knock out large chunks of shrubbery.

• **Home Zoo.** Our impressive collection of stuffed animals kept growing well after the arrival of our daughter, despite our best efforts to let some of the animals "escape." Every time we'd try to donate a few to charity or sell some at a garage sale, Son or Daughter would invariably rescue them and voice their adamant protests that we *couldn't* sell Rocky (the raccoon) or Nip (the kitty) or Butch (the girl dog, so named by three-year-old Madisen).

Not only did the old animals stay, but new ones kept adding to the wildlife population living on the beds and chairs and sofa. One day soon, our home's human inhabitants will doubtless be sitting and sleeping permanently on the floor.

• **Li'l Office.** I actually liked this item after I got over the initial foreboding when it came to us in a big box from one relative or another. It was a rocker-style setup with a wraparound chair (just like Daddy's office chair), a rack of buttons and keys (just like Daddy's computer keyboard), and a built-in pacifier attached to a string (just like Daddy wished he had when late on deadlines).

As one working from a home office and thus facing the occasional challenge of taking daytime charge of the children along with tackling pressing deadlines, I found the Li'l Office to be a fun and helpful attention occupier. And my kids played with it, too. They especially liked to make such a racket with the squeaking buttons and clacking keys that Daddy would have to quit working and focus all his attention on *them.*

• **Cellular Phones.** We inexplicably collected several

of these toy flip-phones that looked and sounded re-
markably like the real thing—so real that we'd sometimes discover, in the car 20 miles from home, that the
working phone was back on the dining room table and
we were trying to dial a number on something that
kept playing "Twinkle, Twinkle, Little Star." The toy
phones were also good for faking people out by pretending that real calls were coming in.

I enjoyed playing that trick on houseguests, until the
time a guest played that trick on me. Someone handed
me a ringing toy in the presence of a number of
friends, and I kept saying "Hello?...Hello?" into it for
several moments before realizing that everyone in the
room was on the verge of rupturing themselves with
laughter.

• **Legos.** Today these come in every conceivable
shape and dimension, from bricks seemingly the size of
cinder blocks to pieces with the approximate propor-
tions of smallish molecules. After two kids we've collected quite a few of them. Sometimes Mommy has to
scold, wading through wall-to-wall Legos in the living
room, "Didn't I tell you to pick these things up?"

"Awww, do I have to?" is my usual reply. "I'm not
finished building things yet!"

Though I joke that kid stuff fills our house—and at
times it's definitely seemed like the case—we have tried
to maintain a bit of sanity about the kinds and amounts
of toys we keep around. Without question my children
have far more than I did, just as I had far more than my
parents did.

Funny thing, though. Some of the most endearing
and enduring playthings my children have taken up are
exactly the items I remember enjoying as a child.
Things like sticks, rocks, sand, boxes, bugs, bubbles,
water, paints, crayons, paper airplanes and many other
items that are readily available and cost little or nothing. This tells me that despite all trends to the contrary,
children (and adults for that matter) don't really need

fancy toys to be happy—except maybe for Legos. And even these aren't as important as some other kid stuff to keep around the house.

• **Time Builder.** When I was a new parent, back in the heyday of the "Quality Time versus Quantity Time" debate, someone gave me the best piece of parenting advice I've ever received. "Don't be fooled," he said. "Quality Time   Quantity Time." In a day when many parents seem to spend so little time with their children between work and lessons and activities and entertainment opportunities, building time with my kids has to be more important than building their toy collections.

• **Priority Bouncer.** In my mind I sometimes need to gather up all those seemingly competing priorities and (to quote Tigger from *Winnie the Pooh*) "bounce 'em out." Sift the truly weighty ones from those that only seem important at the moment. What is a TV playoff game, for instance, compared to a family board game or an outing in the park? I need to bounce that TV—or whatever hollow distraction might come—out of the picture.

• **Attention Button.** It can be hard, in our busy age, to focus on the moment. In that sense maybe my children were on to something, punching those noisy Li'l Office buttons that definitely got my attention. That's what I often need—an "attention button" to bring me back to the present when worries and concerns about the future take my mind away from the people around me right now.

• **Fun Phone.** What I could really use, it seems to me, is a flip phone that neither fakes me out nor connects me with the world. I need one that rings from time to time to tell me, "Lighten up!" Parents today feel so much pressure to do everything right and to soberly bear the massive mantle of parental responsibility. We need regular reminders that it's all right to have a good time.

As a fairly new, somewhat stressed father, I once

asked the parents of several grown children about the dedication and sacrifice it must have taken to raise such fine young adults. With a smile, one of them replied, "We did work at it, but overall I'd say it was more fun than work."

I thought, *of course.* Kids aren't just a lot of work, they're also a lot of fun! It's a lesson for all parents in our age of high anxiety. Half the work of parenting is learning to enjoy it.

Some Assembly Required
(I Wish)

Times have changed since the days when one spouse brought home the bacon and the other spouse cleaned up the grease. Most modern couples share both breadwinning and homemaking responsibilities. At home many of us practice a casual "50/50" rule in which we try to spread around the household tasks and chores fairly evenly.

There is one area of household responsibility, however, that has shown very little progress, if any, towards becoming an equally shared duty between husbands and wives. I'm surprised it hasn't gotten more publicity. What I'm talking about is "Some Assembly Required." In the vast majority of cases, it is the husband's responsibility, and the husband's responsibility alone, to slide those 20 to 200 individual parts out of the box and figure out, with directions badly translated from the original Latin, how Bar A secures to Joint B with Bolt C. And so on. Most wives I know, including my own, show no inclination whatsoever to take part in the "Some Assembly Required" process.

And I don't blame them a bit. Given the challenges of the assembly-required scenario, I'd avoid it, too, if I could. But that's getting harder and harder to do these days. Especially, for those of us who are husbands and fathers and homeowners, the "Some Assembly Required" cloud always lurks ominously on the horizon.

Not long ago I had an interesting experience related to that. I happened to mention to a few friends that I'd recently spent a long Saturday putting together one of those complicated assemble-it-yourself entertainment armoires. To my surprise, the guys gave a collective groan and offered words of support and condolence.

We got to talking about our various Some Assembly Required trials and tribulations. Later it got my imagination working. What if there was a weekly Some Assembly Required support group full of harried husbands and dads...?

I'd been attending my local Assembly-Required Group (ARG!) for a couple of months, but I hadn't really had a whole lot to say yet. In general, everything had been going all right. Other than a minor setback involving the proper connection and operation of a new computer printer, the Some Assembly Required front had been fairly quiet lately.

But one night there was a new guy in the group—I'll call him Bob—and he didn't look good. As a number of us shared some minor do-it-yourself frustrations from the week, Bob kept trembling and teetering on the verge of tears. Finally our leader asked him, "Would you like to share?"

He nodded and stood. "I'm Bob," he said, "and I survived Some Assembly Required." Then he told his story. As in all these cases, it started innocently enough. At his young son's birthday party there was an ominous-looking package, Bob explained, "a big rectangular one that gave a sinister warning rattle when we moved it." The rest of us shuddered. "I tried to laugh it off, to put it out of my mind. But it just didn't feel right."

The party proceeded without incident, Bob continued, and his misgivings subsided a bit. But later while little Robert was opening presents, a voice rang out: "Save the Big One for last!" Bob nearly dropped his camera and felt himself starting to panic. The Big One! Should he dive on top of it? Whisk his son out of harm's way? But it was too late. Robert was already ripping the box open and suddenly, there it was in plain sight.

By then we all knew what it was. Merely the most

terrifying Some Assembly Required item of them all. But Bob had to say it anyway, for his own good. "It was," he rasped, "a swing set."

Though we already knew, it still hurt. Especially me. I must have involuntarily doubled over to catch my breath, because the next thing I knew my neighbor was kneeling beside me asking if I was OK. The leader noticed and inquired, after I'd straightened back up, "Do you have something you need to share as well?"

Reluctantly I stood up and forced myself to admit that I had also recently experienced a birthday swing-set incident. "But mine was worse," I said. Eyebrows raised and gazes intensified. "In my case," I confessed, "I bought the swings myself, entirely on purpose!"

A collective gasp nearly sucked all the air out of the room. Then I began my story: "Everything was going well that day. The weather was beautiful and the party went off without a hitch. As in Bob's case, we saved the Big One for last. I was so naive that the box's warning rattles hadn't alarmed me. And even after my son excitedly tore open the box, the tangle of parts spilling out only caused momentary concern. After all, there *were* instructions."

This caused a wave of sardonic laughter. But it turned quickly to dismay when I added, "Soon I made my critical mistake. I casually mentioned to my son, 'After the party we'll put the set together so you can swing right away.'"

Swing right away! The group could hardly believe I'd said it—yet we'd all said something like it at one time or another. We'd believed that Some Assembly Required really meant "some." We'd trusted the instructions would actually help. We'd assumed putting it together would only require the recommended screwdriver and adjustable wrench. We'd casually commented, "It'll be done in an hour, tops."

Well, the outcome of the story, as I told the group, was that I worked on the set all afternoon. Around dinnertime my son wandered out, surveyed the scene, and asked, "When are you going to start putting together the swings, Daddy?" Then I worked on the set all evening. Upon checking my progress again, Seth frowned and said, "Did you have to take it all apart again or something?" Then I worked on it into the night, until my flashlight batteries went dead and I sat there whimpering in the dark. How symbolic.

When I finished my lament, others chimed in with their own sordid tales of assembling (and failing to assemble) their children's swing sets, play houses, bicycles, basketball hoops and other items. That's when another new guy—I'll call him Brad—piped up and said, "You people are pathetic."

We looked around, somewhat stunned.

"All this whining about putting together a few toys," Brad continued. "What kind of men are you? What in the world has manhood come to?"

We all began to clear our throats and hang our heads in shame, but our leader just smiled and asked, "And how many children do you have, Brad?"

"Well," Brad replied, "none yet. But my wife is due any day. I'm going home right after this meeting to put together the crib."

Ah, the crib. Some Assembly Required. With easy directions. Just a screwdriver and an adjustable wrench needed. Only take an hour, tops.

Everyone brightened at the thought. Brad would be back next week, a wiser man.

Partners in Grime

Though I complain about the messes and stresses and complexities that are inherent in the work of parenting, my wife and I have developed somewhat of a philosophical perspective about the whole thing. We kind of like it. When newlywed or childless acquaintances ask how we're enjoying family life, we invariably bore them to tears with long affectionate narratives about the challenges and rewards of juggling children with careers with church activities with household responsibilities and so on.

But I am proud to say we always refrain from spouting that annoying cliché parents are always splattering on pre-parents: "Your time will come!" I haven't decided if such astonishing presumption comes from hormone changes triggered by having kids or simply from brain-wear due to juggling children with careers with church activities with household responsibilities and so on.

On the downside, since we don't immediately scare newlywed and childless couples away with the "Your time will come!" line, the child-free folks have to endure our dishing of dirt about diapers, dishes and other messy details of modern family life. I remember one couple perking up recently, however, when we mentioned we had shipped the kids to Grampa and Gramma's in order to enjoy an intimate evening at home.

"Ah," they said, winking and flicking their eyebrows. "And how did you enjoy that?"

"It was great," Kim replied. "We got the bathtub clean."

"Woa," the newlyweds said with sly grins, "kinky!"

"No," I said, "I think we used Comet. Hon, did we use Comet or Ajax to clean the bathtub that night?"

The couple's eyes glazed over again as we lovingly

recalled our wonderful evening of cleaning the house without the kids rendering it meaningless 30 seconds later. After we said our good-byes, I think I heard one of them whisper to the other, "Maybe children are over-rated."

Actually, not at all. Kim and I didn't know anything about relating until we had kids. During a dozen years of marriage, our relationship expectations have changed. Thankfully. Before children, for instance, you might have found us planning, say, the Perfect Ski Weekend. In our minds it might have gone something like this:

Friday 6 A.M.: Leave for mountains.

Friday 9 A.M.: Hit the slopes.

Friday 6 P.M.: Check into Lodge.

Friday 9 P.M.: Enjoy roaring fire after dinner and hot tub.

Saturday 9 A.M.: Hit the slopes.

Saturday 6 P.M.: Dinner, hot tub, roaring fire, etc…

At least that would have been the plan. In reality it probably would have gone more like this:

Friday 6 A.M.: Can't find other half of ski rack.

Friday 7 A.M.: Find other half, but of course have no idea now where first half is.

Friday 9 A.M.: After locating both halves and finally getting out of town, drive back home to actually put skis on rack.

Friday 1 P.M.: Hit slopes after inching to mountains through a blizzard, three traffic jams and an hour figuring out how to put on the tire chains.

Friday 3 P.M.: Wait in endless lift line for second run of the day.

Friday 3:15 P.M.: Lift stalls halfway up due to high winds, while spouse digs fingernails through three layers of sleeve as chair blows at 90 degree angle high above slopes.

Friday 6 P.M.: Lodge has no record of reservations.

Friday 11 P.M.: After finally working out reservations, waiting an hour for dinner to arrive, settling into a hot tub we quickly learn it is out of order at 52 degrees and building a roaring fire to warm up, we peer through thick smoke to realize fireplace damper is labeled incorrectly and currently "closed" rather than "open."

Saturday 9 A.M.: More of same…

Granted, our Perfect Ski Weekends and other childless outings weren't always so spectacularly short of perfect, but it was only after we started raising a family that we learned why we sometimes came home dissatisfied. At those times, we realized, we were counting more on our circumstances to bring us pleasure than our relationship.

After kids, that all changed. We even gave up skiing soon after our son was born because of a single overriding realization: there was no way we could fit both the ski stuff and baby stuff in the car.

But we didn't regret it. What a relief to quit seeking the elusive Perfect Ski Weekend and start planning, say, the Imperfect Beach Weekend:

Friday 8 A.M.: Decide to try and leave for beach by 9 A.M. Then laugh hysterically at the good joke we've made, knowing that with children we'll be lucky to get out of town by noon.

Friday 10 A.M.: Attempt first of several "trunk stompings" to try and jam in all the clothes, toys, floaters, towels, balls, coolers, portable cribs, beach chairs, snacks and plethora of other items we're taking.

Friday 11 A.M.: Get on road and congratulate ourselves for leaving an hour early, Kid Time.

Friday 1 P.M.: Arrive at beach and discover weather is cloudy and cool. "Should we go back home?" one of us asks, at which point we again laugh hysterically at the good joke we've made, because the kids couldn't care less if it's cloudy and cool, as long as they can play in the sand.

Friday 6 P.M.: After several hours of sandy fun,

check into lodge which, not being run by painfully hip ski people, has our reservations.

Sunday 6 P.M.:   After beach-intensive weekend, arrive home to unload kids and luggage and transfer them directly to backyard sand box to shake out two or three barrels of sand.

Next 3 days: Vacuum sand out of car.

Yet even with its imperfections, if you would ask later how our weekend went, we would likely tell you, "Perfect!"   Our children have taught us that grime is our friend.   The messy stuff—and here I'm talking about more than dirt—isn't a distraction from the relationship, it the relationship.

That's why, if I answer "Great" when somebody asks how my Saturday went, I'm probably not referring to my golf score.   Or my skiing or fishing or softball playing or any other officially sanctioned avenue of fun.   If I say my Saturday was great, it may well mean that we finally got a chance to pitch in together to clean out the garage.   Or pull weeds and trim bushes.   Or clean up our rooms (especially Daddy).   Or simply play in our recently replenished sandbox all day.

And for those freewheeling folks who may pity our boring existence, don't waste your sympathy on us.   Because in the simple joy of family life we have discovered the greatest pleasure of all: no more searching for the other half of that blamed ski rack.

World's Slowest Parent

In certain aspects of parenting and household management, I've noticed, my wife can do things much faster than I can. She is, for example, a supermarket whiz. "I have to get a few things from the store," she'll say, then about 70 seconds later will walk back in the door.

"Forget something?" I'll ask.

"Uh, no," she'll reply. "I had to get a few things from the store." And sure enough, she'll be toting a couple of bags of groceries into the kitchen.

How does she do that?

I'm not nearly so speedy when I go to the store. When I'm heading out the door for that purpose, Kim will sometimes say, "Don't forget to write!" Har har.

But it's true. I'm slow. Or perhaps more accurately, I'm distractible. Sending me out to the store is like dispatching that kid Billy on an errand in comic. I track loopy dotted lines over half the county.

Some might take this as another one of those gender things. Women are naturally domestic, while men are domestically dim. Aren't men always wandering around trying to find their socks, especially when they're stored in mysterious places such as the dresser drawer where they belong? Well, I don't know about other men, but that's not how it is for me. I generally know the whereabouts of my socks (or at least one of each pair) and am fairly handy in most domestic matters. But I do tend to be overly methodical and occasionally absent-minded. In the complex world of home and family, such traits can cause the life of a naturally slow person to become practically glacial.

The grocery store problem illustrates the nature of my slowness. It starts when I realize, pulling in to the parking lot, that I've forgotten the checkbook. Back home I drive, only to discover that Kim and the kids have gone to visit a neighbor and have locked me out. At that point I realize my house key is lying conveniently on my desk, which of course is locked conveniently in the house. So I rummage through the neighborhood looking for Kim, and finally get her key to let myself in. Grabbing my own key, I notice that I've also forgotten a couple of coupons on my desk. I pocket the coupons, head out the door, and on the way back to the store drive by to give Kim her key.

"So you got the checkbook?" Kim asks. I almost slap my forehead, but manage to restrain myself. Years of forgetfulness finally forced me into Deslap, so I wouldn't keep knocking precious brain cells out of my head every time something is left at home.

Anyway, I go back to get the checkbook and finally head to the store with everything in order—house keys, coupons, checkbook, shopping list—er, shopping list. Hmm. Gotta be around here somewhere. Pockets? Nope. Glove compartment? Nope. Back seat? Nope. Car-vaulting pedestrian I'm about to hit? Nope. Oh well. I can probably remember what was on the list.

As I try to drag the list contents from the recesses of my memory bank, it slowly dawns on me that I passed the store at least five minutes ago. And somehow the road, entirely without my knowledge, has schlepped me onto the Interstate by the big sign that says **Next Exit: 7 Miles**.

How could I do this *again?* I grumblingly drive the seven miles and swerve up the off ramp past Jeb's Gas 'n' Store, where Jeb gives a familiar smile and wave, and swerve down the onramp and grumbingly drive the seven miles back. There I squeal into the grocery store parking lot and realize I should have used part of that 14 miles to think of what was on my shopping list rather than grumbling.

I shuffle into the store mumbling "Milk, bread, cereal, bananas..." and so on, proceeding to employ my foolproof shopping system of trying to put as much store as possible between me and the next item I need. Finally I wheel up to the checkout line and discover once again that I'm right behind the person with 692 coupons for the checker to laboriously scan. When I finally arrive home, seemingly hours later, Kim gives me her routine astonished look and says, "You're back earlier than usual!"

This is how it is for me. Mostly I can live with being slow (it actually has its advantages for a writer, which is an inherently slow occupation) but sometimes it can be a pain. Especially in the pursuit of parenting, which is already the slowest job on earth.

When I say "slow" I don't mean "dull," of course. Workaholics and jet setters who think that those on the "mommy track" or "daddy track" are missing out on life simply don't know what they're talking about. Far from being dull, parenting is demanding and lively and unpredictable every waking second, and even many sleeping seconds. But it does take extreme amounts of time. Unbelievable amounts of time. At least it does for me. Solar systems form in less time than it takes for me to feed my children breakfast.

It used to seem that way, anyway. Things have gotten better with experience and with my children's growing independence. But there was a time when the gap between my wife's efficiency and my own deficiency seemed huge. She could get the kids ready, feed them breakfast, have their teeth brushed and hair combed, and involve them in constructive activities in about the time it took me to locate the light switches in their rooms. For Kim getting the children dressed was elementary; for me it was advanced trigonometry. What shirt went with which pants? Or skirt with shoes? Where were the shirts and pants and skirts and shoes in the first place? Which of those 75 hair bows, clips, bands, berets and other tress-control devices would I use for my daughter's hair? For someone who already had enough trouble deciding whether to eat Cheerios or Wheaties in the morning, these dozens of additional parenting choices could be mind-boggling. And that's still the case to some degree. My natural slowness slows me down even more in the low-speed world of parenting.

Over time (of course) I've decided this isn't such a bad thing. In our fast-lane culture we need to slow down to our children's leisurely pace more often. Obviously one needs to strike a balance here—many tasks and responsibilities do require speed and punctuality—but sometimes we simply go too fast for our children's good. Or ours. Kids don't see each moment as something to rush through on the way to the next. Not everything has to be efficient. Sometimes efficiency kills significance.

So being slow has its good points. It still drives me crazy in the store when I'm on aisle 2 and the last item I need is on aisle 31; or when Kim has informed me that my daughter needs to wear "that yellow shirt" and I end up spending an hour puzzling over nine varieties of yellow shirt in the drawer. But when slowness knocks me off my sacred "To Do" list occasionally to play catch or hide-and-seek at the expense of getting things done faster, that's OK. Someday my memory bank will have only so much room to store the rich stock of recollections from "the good old days" when we were young, fun-loving parents. Will I remember getting something (or anything) done on time, or will I remember that great game of catch or hide-and-seek that stretched into a warm summer evening?

You don't have to be too quick to know the answer.

Teaching the Teacher

When my turn came to give sage advice to the expectant parents at a couple's baby shower, I rather surprised myself with my own words. Apparently I didn't really know that I knew what I knew. Or something like that. At any rate, what I said was, "Don't obsess about doing everything right. Your child will let you know what to do."

Well, maybe I did know that I knew that, but it's easy to forget in a day when parents feel so much pressure to be perfect leaders and nurturers of their children. One false move, we think, and they're scarred for life. Of course we parents do need to be conscientious teachers and modelers of good behavior for our kids. But I also learned early on that my children would often be teachers and modelers of good behavior for me. Given most children's unhurried and unworried approach to life, no wonder Jesus said that "the kingdom of God belongs to such as these."

Parenting is a learning experience from the start, but I didn't necessarily expect my young children to lecture me in the lessons of life so directly. For me that started one spring afternoon when my oldest was only a toddler. As we walked into the backyard to play, Seth surveyed the lawn and said, "Look at all the pretty flowers!" They were dandelions. Though this is a common (and perhaps cliched) theme, that a parent's weeds are a child's wildflowers, it was a new thought for me. It opened my eyes to all kinds of ways Seth seemed to have a more gracious, expansive worldview than I did.

At first when we'd take walks or bike rides around the block, for instance, I would subconsciously try to turn them into exercise opportunities, worry sessions or other "purposeful" excursions. But Seth would always take his own sweet time and veer off this way or that,

forcing me to pay attention to more immediate sensa-
tions. "See the birdies?" he'd ask. "Look at that tree.
The sky is pretty! These flowers smell nice." Seth
knew the right things to pay attention to, even if his
distracted daddy didn't.

Then there were the times I'd be occupying a Saturday afternoon planted, say, in front of a crucial TV golf
tournament I just had to doze through...I mean watch.
Seth would invariably sidle up with a stack of books
and urge, "Daddy, read?" My son, the media critic. I'd
thought I was the one designated to lecture my kids on
reading more and watching TV less, not the other way
around.

As Seth grew older he only grew more astute. One
time when his mommy and I were reprimanding him
rather loudly for something I can't remember now—
which tells you how important it must have been—Seth
covered his ears with a cringe and protested, "You're
talking so loud I can't hear you!" Genius. It's become
a family motto: Don't talk so loud that we can't hear
each other.

By kindergarten Seth had taught me a life-changing
message about time. This was when "*Carpe Diem*" was
a big men's movement item—seize the day, make the
most of every opportunity and all that. So when it was
my turn to pick up Seth from school, I'd tend to "*Carpe
Diem*" us right back home so I could "seize the deadline" and "make the most stress of every opportunity."
This caused Seth tremendous frustration. He always
wanted to play in the school playground a bit with a
few other after-school regulars who were either less
time-driven or better at persuading their time-driven
parents to take a load off for a few minutes.

Finally one afternoon when I answered Seth's pleas
yet again with, "Not today," he asked, "Why not?" Turns
out it was a pretty good question. Why not indeed? I
couldn't take 10 minutes to enjoy the fresh air and laughing children? It suddenly occurred to me that in this

case, "making the most of an opportunity" was right here in this playground, not back at a piled-up desk.

Seth continues to teach me as much as I teach him, and my youngest is continuing the tradition. Like Seth did before her, she seems to know what's good for Daddy better than Daddy does. She gets me to work in the morning ("Time to wake up, Daddy!"), roots me from the sofa on weekends ("Let's go outside."), and reminds me to exercise ("Want to go for a bike ride?"). She urges me to value relationships ("I need you to help me."), promotes family closeness ("Want a hug and a kiss?"), and forces me to relax ("Come play with me!"). Those who say that children need good parents only have it half right. Good parents need their children to help them get there.

The prophet Isaiah wasn't kidding when he said, "a little child will lead them." Some of the greatest lessons my kids have taught me have been spiritual. One Sunday after services awhile back, Seth said to me, "I liked church today. It was good." That launched me into my usual mental analysis of the morning—what I liked and didn't like about the service and other activities. But my little mentor interrupted my musings with the question, "And do you know what the best thing is?"

I asked what.

"The best thing is that God is good," Seth pronounced. "I love God. He's better than anything."

Whew! Talk about busting Daddy for his critical spirit and getting to the heart of the matter.

But this was nothing new. Seth had been nailing me from the time he could barely talk. When I tell you that we pray every night before bed, I want to stress that it's not because of some great parental commitment or farreaching spiritual vision on my part. It's because Seth, as a mere two-year old, roundly convicted me on the subject one night when I was depositing him in his crib.

Mommy was out for the evening and Daddy had

been taking care of things—with no little help from Seth. Every time I began to scratch my head about what to do next, he toddled up with a book or snack or pair of pajamas, or perhaps with a pertinent question like, "Drink of water?" As we made our way to the bedroom to get him tucked in, I began feeling pretty smug about how well the whole evening had gone.

For only a moment. As I covered him up and turned out the light, Seth had one more thing to say. "Daddy pray?"

Oh yeah.

Thank goodness for children. *Somebody* has to remember the important stuff.

PART FOUR

Males and Females

Working It Out

Working Hard or Hardly Working?

Once in a while when I greet a friend or acquaintance, the person will give me a wink and quip, "Are you working hard or hardly working?" I never know how to answer. Either reply, it seems, can get a person in trouble:

Me: "I'm working hard."

They: "Oh, so you're not spending time with your family?"

Me: "I mean I'm hardly working."

They: "Oh, so you're not taking care of your family?"

Me: "Uh, neither. I mean both. I mean...what was the question again?"

In reality I'm a bit wobbly on the line between working hard and hardly working. Which only means I'm normal. Today's culture has a tough time with work and rest. One minute we're chastised for being too obsessed with work, and the next minute we're scolded for being too lazy to work. It's enough to cause a chronic twitch. Working hard? Take a break, get some rest, go on vacation! Hardly working? Get busy, don't waste time, there are a million things to do!

That's the struggle of daily life. We look forward to 5 P.M. so we can finally get out of our meetings to rush home, scarf down dinner and rush out to more meetings. We look forward to weekends so we can get away from work to do more work. Let's see, this weekend let's clean house, do laundry, paint the garage, remodel the bathroom, bus the kids around to music rehearsals and sports practices, get the shopping done, wash the car and change the oil, re-landscape the back yard, host a barbecue, go to the mountains, attend a wedding, get a head start on those Monday deadlines, catch up on devotions, and lead and/or attend a full schedule of church activities.

Then let's go back to work to rest up from our days off.

Somewhere along the line, in the midst of all the rushing around, there may come a time when we decide we're tired of living this way. We need to cut back. So we cross everything off the weekend schedule to sway on the hammock and read a good book. Between pages, though, nagging reminders keep flitting by. Do I need to clean the gutters? What about those weeds in the flowerbeds? That wobbly dining room chair needs gluing. And what if it rains before I get the trim painted? About then the neighbor mows by in his yard and gives a small wave and glance that say, "Must be nice to lie around contributing to the decline of civilization."

Up and at 'em!

My wife also struggles with this. Occasionally she will declare to me, "That's it, I'm beat. I'm going to sit down and read my book, and I don't care what doesn't get done." Good for her. When she says that I always encourage, "Great idea, go for it, you should do that more often," and so on. Like most people these days (and women in particular) she tries to take on too much.

Yet, later, when I ask her if she enjoyed putting her feet up for awhile, she'll often frown and reply, "No, I kept thinking about what I wasn't getting done."

I can relate. Even when I'm trying to successfully balance the conflicting calls of "work harder" and "take it easier" in my mind, it doesn't always work out in reality. Perhaps after a number of days in a row of working extra hours I'll decide to compensate by taking an afternoon off to play golf. There I'll be on the first tee, surveying the beautiful scenery, taking a slow, steady backswing, and...hmm. *Did I call Norm back?* I'll wonder. *He was waiting for that information. If I didn't call Norm, he can't call Darrel, and Darrel can't call*

Clara, and Clara can't call Merrill, and Merrill can't call me. At that point I'll be going into my downswing and *clank*, the ball will shoot sideways off my driver, thwack a tree, ricochet off a bench and scatter the foursome waiting to tee off behind me. As they recover and glare at me, I explain, "Forgot to call Norm." They say "Ah" understandingly, a couple of them giving a start and yanking out cell phones to contact people *they* forgot to call.

Then back at work, it will go the other way. I'll be writing an e-mail, and suddenly the thought will fly into my mind, *I should have kept my head down. I was looking up too soon and taking my eye off the ball during my swing. That's why I kept duffing my wedges around the green.*

A little while later I'll receive a return e-mail that says, "Got your message that we need to change the wording in the introductory paragraph to avoid duffing our wedges around the green. Please explain." But I don't really have an explanation. Why I go out to the golf course to worry about work, and then go back to the office to worry about my golf game, I don't know.

With all this weekly working hard versus hardly working confusion, I find it fortunate that more serious times off come around occasionally, days on which one is supposed to take a rest. Holidays and vacations provide more time and opportunity than evenings and weekends to consider ways to relax and recreate—and then ignore relaxation and recreation, of course, in order to take on even bigger projects.

In recent years I've come to wonder if our culture has become holiday impaired. At Christmas time, for example, we tend to celebrate the simple, humble birth of Jesus by trying to make the holiday as extravagant, complicated and stressful as possible. Then at New Years we commemorate the hope and promise of a fresh 12 months by obsessing about all the failures and bad habits that need changing from the last 12 months.

Around Easter many of us celebrate resurrection and new life by attending and/or performing in an entire range of late and early church services, possibly followed by eating enough chocolate eggs and bunnies to make us feel like we may have one foot in the grave. Labor Day may be the most aptly-named holiday of all, since we commemorate labor by laboring like crazy trying to complete all those unfinished summer projects before a new season of school and work responsibilities begins. Other holidays entice us into similar patterns. Rather than resting up from a job well done, we're tempted to tackle all the tasks that still need starting.

Vacations aren't always better. The concept of lying around doing nothing on vacation seems rather quaint and archaic. The object now appears to be how much you can do, how much you can see, how many places you can go and most importantly, how much money you can spend. It amazes me how much work people go to these days to get away from work.

Some say we live in an age that no longer values working hard, but I wonder if it's equally true that we no longer understand hardly working. So work and rest continue to jam together in a never-ending quandary: Am I working hard or hardly working? To get anywhere in life, I have to work hard. But to enjoy life, I have to take it easy. To make a living, though, I have to work hard. But to keep living, I have to take it easy. And on it goes.

If anyone out there knows how to balance the two, please give me a ring. You can reach me on the golf course getting stressed about the office, or possibly in the office getting stressed about my golf game.

How Very Busy People Get Everything Done (In Our Dreams)

Given our ongoing struggle with working hard versus hardly working, my wife and I try to keep alert for tips and wisdom about how to fit everything in. Awhile ago we clipped an article from a small-business newsletter titled *How Very Busy People Manage Their Time.* That got our attention. We are indeed Very Busy Persons.

But not, I should add, because we're particularly brilliant or important or in-demand, as are many other VBPs. If you ask me, being brilliant or important or in-demand sounds like a lot of work. A much easier way to stay Very Busy, we've found, is to consistently apply the principle of ED (Extreme Disorganization). ED is a great way to make a little bit of work highly demanding and stressful, just like important work done by important people.

Still, ED has its downside, which I'd tell you about if I could find the paper on which I wrote it down. So, as I said, we try to keep alert for ways to get BO. I mean Better Organized.

To that end, the article I mentioned shares time-management tips from three Very Busy People who *are* brilliant, important and in-demand, and I can see why. From their advice, I gather these VBPs get a tremendous amount of work done each day while still finding quality time for their families, communities and charitable organizations. One VBP, whom I will call Joe Author, has written more than a dozen books and gives 100 speeches a year. How does he do it all? Here are some highlights:

- Prioritizes all responsibilities for the day as A (urgent), B (important) or C (can wait).
- Keeps a clean desk, not letting paperwork pile up.
- Delegates tasks to his 10-person staff.
- Sets long-term goals and strives each day to do one thing toward reaching them.

Reading these tips, I was struck with a profound insight: where does a writer get a 10-person staff? As a fellow writer, I can barely afford to pay myself. With a 10-person staff, I could probably get more done too. It would be much easier, for instance, to move the desk around under my computer mouse to get that pointy thing to shift positions on the monitor. I'm sure Kim wouldn't at all mind having a 10-person staff either. Not necessarily for her work, which she manages very well all by herself, but for a little household help. Ten people picking up after our two young children sounds like about the right ratio.

Beyond our zero-person staff, though, I suppose Joe Author's other tips could be helpful. Long-term goals sound nice. The times I've written long-term goals in my journal to start the year, I've always been fortunate to look back on those goals at year's end and realize that I've misplaced the journal pages and no longer have to worry about whether I've met them or not.

And a clean desk. I found a clean desk to be very efficient, not to mention white (I'd forgotten what my desktop looked like) the one time I had one—when the threat of flooding in my neighborhood forced me to dump foot-high stacks of papers and files into boxes to clear them out in case of water damage.

I'm not so sure about the prioritizing of commitments and responsibilities, though. What's urgent? What can wait? For a writer, it seems like writing would be urgent. But many authors will tell you that when they sit down to write, writing suddenly becomes the farthest thing from their minds. Facing a particular piece of writing, other pressing demands invariably assault the brain. *What's this annoying piece of something stuck between my upper right molars?* we wonder, and *Is a semicolon really punctuation or is it a medical condition?* There's nothing like sitting down to meet a writing deadline to get the creative juices flowing.

But my impression is that when Joe Author sits down to write, he actually writes. And he calls himself a writer.

The second VBP interviewed in the *How Very Busy People Manage Their Time* article is someone I'll call Jane Doctor. Ms. D suggests the following:
Use a pocket electronic organizer to keep track of your schedule.
Make sure that everything you do gives you pleasure or satisfaction.
Set aside time for exercise.
Leave time for a rich family life.

Right away, I see a problem. Using an electronic organizer—one of those little calculator-like gadgets with keys the size of pinheads—would not give me pleasure or satisfaction. Just finger cramps. So that means Jane Doctor's first two tips cancel each other out. And though I firmly believe in exercise (to the point where I've actually considered doing it upon occasion) and I do leave time for a rich family life (which does give me extreme pleasure and satisfaction) how are these going to help me write the column due today or the chapters due next week?

I realize Jane Doctor is talking long-term health and sanity here, and I commend her for it. But if we're going to get BO, er, Better Organized, we probably need more practical advice.

The final Very Busy Person interviewed in the article is someone I'll call John Financial Adviser. Mr. Finance says he works every day from 4 A.M. to 4 P.M. so his evenings will be free for precious family time. I can just imagine this Very Important Family Man's schedule:
4 A.M. to 4 P.M.—work

4:30 to 6:30—Music lessons, sports practices, play dates and other after-school activities.
6:30 to 7—Make dinner.
7 to 8—Family meal around dinner table.
8 to 9—Games or activities with kids.
9 to 10—Cleanup, laundry, household chores and repairs.
10 to 11—Exercise and/or unwind.
11 to 12—Meaningful conversation with wife.
3 A.M.—Wake up (!) and get ready for work.

Granted, I may be exaggerating here. As a multimillionaire, Mr. Finance may well hire people to chauffeur, cook, clean up, do laundry, fix things, and possibly to have meaningful conversations with his wife. Then again, perhaps John has come up with The Perfect Schedule, just the thing to change an EDVBP (Extremely Disorganized Very Busy Person) like me into a VIVBP (Very Important Very Busy Person).

I can see it all now. I would go to work at 4 A.M. (finally waking up enough around 8 to get something meaningful done), and knock off at 4 P.M. Then (after stopping at Starbucks for coffee, extra strong) I'd taxi the kids around to their various activities until 6:30 P.M. After putting together dinner, my wife and I would gather our little brood around the dining room table at 7 P.M. and bow our heads to give thanks. Then, sitting there peacefully in my chair, I could take some time to truly reflect on the blessings of life and the fruit of my labor.

Snoring, face down in the lasagna.

What We Need,
We Probably Don't Need

In the working world, one of the complimentary temptations to finding the perfect schedule can be acquiring the perfect equipment. At least it's a temptation for me. I wouldn't consider myself to be a materialistic person by nature, but I do have an odd weakness for office supplies. Where others might salivate over sports cars or speedboats, I gaze longingly at sticky notes.

Fortunately my wife is a pragmatist when it comes to office equipment, so I generally run potential purchases through her. Not that Kim doesn't have her own materialistic enticements. A running joke between us is her status as a "bag lady"—one who has a strange compulsion to collect all manner of handbags and totes and duffels and luggage items, far more than she could ever use at any one time. But that doesn't carry over to office supplies, where her philosophy is unequivocally "Only what we need." Killjoy.

I've been wary of pronouncing certain kinds of phenomena "gender things," but in this case I think it just might be. Why do some men outfit their entire garages with professional shop equipment for the sole purpose of sanding down an edge once in a while? Because tools are neat. Why do men collect expensive golf apparatus in order to become more powerful and proficient at whacking balls into the woods? Because golf clubs are cool.

Of course, it may be an overstatement to claim office supplies are "cool" like tools and golf clubs. I may be the only one who thinks so. Still, I will admit to sometimes flipping through office warehouse catalogs and dreaming about what my "perfect office" might be like...

Dream: To get the latest, greatest computer system with all the options such as the most memory, fastest chip, biggest hard drive, widest monitor, nimblest modem, newest recordable CD drive and so on, in order to dramatically increase the speed and efficiency of my work.

Reality: The latest, greatest computer system would do little or nothing to increase the speed and efficiency of my work. The modest computer I currently use is already more powerful than I really need, sitting here doing the glacially slow work of writing and editing. I suspect my computer rather champs at the bit from time to time, thinking, "Give me something harder to do than sitting here waiting while you ponder whether to type "their" or "they're.""

I did have occasion recently to consider forking out for a new system, though, when a modem problem started to hinder the sending and receiving of e-mail. "Modem's not working right," I ventured. "Might be a good time to replace this old computer."

"How much?" Kim asked.

"Only two thousand."

"How much for a new modem?"

"Uh, 49 bucks."

"Go," Kim said, "with a new modem."

Well sure, if I want the dissatisfaction of doing the *smart* thing.

Dream: To buy a multifunction office machine that prints, scans, faxes and copies all in one unit, in order to gain more versatility and save precious desk space.

Reality: The separate printer and scanner units I already own not only take up less space than a multifunction machine, but can also print, scan, fax and copy just as well. As compared with a new multifunction machine, however, there is a significant drawback with my current setup: not as many colorful buttons.

Dream: To replace my boring old gray-upholstered desk chair with a soft leather high-back fully adjustable electric-massaging chair, in order to achieve a more comfortable, tranquil, stress-free bearing while working on the computer.

Reality: Sit down in chair, turn on the massager and zzzzzzzzzzzz...

Dream: To mount a compact audiovisual setup on the wall for the convenient viewing of work-related videos.

Reality: The number of work-related videos I've been called upon to view in the last five years is exactly two (with one of those being, technically, a collection of Bugs Bunny cartoons).

Dream: To keep a full range of designer printer paper on hand to add splash and dash to a variety of printing jobs.   One I particularly like, for instance, is called GeoCrumpled-Gray, which looks like someone has wadded it up and tried to spread it out again.

Reality: Writers write on white. Nothing drives editors crazier than getting manuscripts with strange formats, silly fonts and weird paper like GeoCrumpled-Gray. I still think it would be fun, however, to print my tax returns or pretend I've found a lost Hemingway manuscript on wadded-up looking paper. At least until I land in jail.

Dream: To install all the trendy new software, such as (to list a few I've actually been getting flyers for lately) a program to add animated cartoon sequences to my computer documents, one to include flames and rotating 3-D words to my e-mail messages, and another for simplifying the search for career-critical Internet websites such as the Elvis Impersonator's Page.

Reality: Though it may be tempting these days to replace actual words and ideas with cartoon sequences, flaming 3-D graphics and technological bells and whistles, I wouldn't feel good about doing it—at least until words become obsolete. Maybe next year.

Dream: To purchase a $119.99 pen I saw, if only to find out what makes it worth $119 more than the pens I usually buy. Perhaps it has special powers, such as built-in creativity.

Reality: Creativity is still a painstaking human process, no matter how much our high-tech age tries to make it otherwise.

Dream: To get a little in-office coffee maker/espresso machine to save me the trouble of trudging all the way to the kitchen to get coffee.

Reality: The trudge from my office to our current kitchen coffee maker is exactly nine steps. Which leads me to conclude that if I think nine steps a long way, I really need to get out more.

Dream: To collect an assortment of other nifty office gadgets shown in the catalogs, such as a pop-up dispenser for sticky notes (saving me a whopping .05 seconds over pulling them off the pad myself), a futuristic stapler that sits upright like a video-game joystick (and stylishly does exactly the same thing as my old cheapie stapler), a retro-style time clock that punches time cards with an emphatic kerCHUNK (not that I use time cards—I just like the kerCHUNK), and a magnetic clip big enough to clamp a dictionary and hang it on the refrigerator (and if you wonder why I'd want to do that, I will quickly assure you I have no idea).

Reality: I don't really need any of this stuff. My job relies far less on the accumulation of office equipment than the activity of my brain. Which may be a scary thought, but it seems even scarier that the rampant growth of high technology has downplayed brain activity as too slow and inefficient. We want everything done *now*, even when it turns out it wasn't really what we wanted done after all because we were too busy wanting it done *now* to think it through.

So I should be thankful that when it comes to wanting the latest office equipment, my wife will usually advise, "One doesn't need that trendy new thing if the dull old thing still does the job." At least I hope she's referring to office equipment. If she's really talking about me, I don't want to know.

Money For Muffing

S tudies show that money is the number one cause of marital strife. That's certainly true in my own marriage. Though my wife and I are classic soul mates—we fell in love at first sight, got engaged six months later and have been inseparable ever since—money is the one thing that can regularly get us steamed. That's partly because we don't have much of it (at least by affluent North American standards), but even more so because neither one of us has much of a head for finances.

This seems odd. We compliment each other in so many other ways. Kim is an extrovert and I'm an introvert, so she helps me be more sociable and I help her pull back for quiet times when she's tempted to cram her social calendar too full. Kim is a doer and I'm a thinker, so she helps me put action to my thoughts when I get hesitant, and I help her think about her actions before she gets ahead of herself. These kinds of complimentary strengths largely abandon us when it comes to handling money, though. To paraphrase an old joke, when they were handing out the money smarts, we apparently were out to lunch.

But we keep working on it. And obviously we're not alone. At times I've assumed that we couples of modest means are most likely to experience financial disagreements, but clearly that's not the case. A few years ago I played golf with a fairly affluent guy who expressed displeasure with his driver as we stood waiting behind a foursome teeing off. Suddenly the man strode purposefully to the clubhouse and a few moments later returned with one of those high-tech oversized drivers that are popular nowadays. Leaning toward the other three of us in our foursome, he confided, "Two hundred bucks. My wife is not going to be happy."

At that point it occurred to me that perhaps I'd been wrong in thinking that people with more money automatically had fewer money troubles. Maybe wealthier folks merely have more money to get into trouble with.

In reality, money stress isn't necessarily tied to the amount of money one has or doesn't have. I know families of modest means who do an excellent job of managing their finances and I know families of expansive resources who struggle to pay the bills every month. It's ironic to note that in the wealthy United States, where more people are making more money than ever before, the general population is also saving less money than ever.

The main reason that saving money has become so hard, of course, is because spending money has become so easy. Especially with so much of the money we're spending these days not being real money, but hypothetical money. Checks, credit cards, electronic transfers and other newfangled payment procedures make money much easier to part with than the old-time practice of handing over cold hard cash. If I had to pay my mortgage with a fat wad of real dollar bills, the bank would probably have to pry them out of my fist with a crowbar.

Real money seems so much easier to hold on to than hypothetical money. Sometimes I drive my wife crazy with this deep-seated reluctance to break up bills. She'll want me to buy her a pack of gum or something, and I'll say, "Well, I only have a twenty."

"So what?" she'll respond, rolling her eyes. "You'll have to spend it sometime."

I suppose, but I hate breaking up a twenty for 59 cents. Which may seem like non-cents, but I have my reasons. I might need that twenty for something important, like bribing passing motorists for a ride when I run out of gas because I was too cheap to break up my twenty to get gas in the first place.

When handling hypothetical money, however, one's

grip can get a bit slippery. The banks don't help.
Every few days they send yet another offer for some
pre-approved credit card: "To receive our fabulous MasterVisaDiscoverCard with a generous $40,000 credit
line, just lean out your window and offer thumbs-up to
our handy passing response plane!" Strange. To get a
loan for our house, which cost less than many new
cars, we practically had to part with several vital or-
gans.   But if we merely accepted all those pre-approved credit card offers that regularly slide through
our mail slot, we could easily run up a mortgage-like
debt.   As someone said, what a great country this is,
where one minute you can have nothing, and the next
minute you can have $40,000 *less.*

Though I moan about some of our financial anxieties,
I should add that Kim and I have never been ones to
drop hypothetical thousands on things that seem to
tempt others, such as fancy cars, designer fashions or
state-of-the-art golf clubs. I can play poorly enough
with my old golf clubs, thank you. Where we seem to
struggle is in the small things. We have some of the
right ideas in theory, I think, but they don't always
translate into solid practice. For example...

- We keep a file marked *Budget* prominently in our financial file bin. Someday we may even work up a
budget to stick in there.

- Before purchasing big-ticket items we always calcu-
late our "price range" to know what figure to absolutely avoid going beyond. Then we often buy the
more expensive item anyway.

- For a number of years we've kept helpful money-
tracking software on our computer. It wasn't until
this year that we actually started using it.

- We promptly write checks for bills upon receipt and
seal them in their return envelopes to mail on the appropriate dates. Then we promptly forget about the
envelopes when they get buried under other stacks
of papers.

• Recently we've been dialoging about the need to cut down on eating out several times a week. Primarily we discuss this while eating out several times a week.

Though annoying habits like these do prove to be problematic from time to time, I suppose our money troubles could be worse. Many of our differences are really more about style than substance. Kim likes to shop around for things to get the best prices, for instance, whereas I find any number of things more pleasurable than shopping—such as having my toenails pulled out with pliers. I like to swing by Starbucks for a mocha from time to time, but Kim thinks espresso drinks are an outrageously overpriced fad, especially when you can get similar flavor for free by drinking battery acid. Kim seems compelled to purchase several varieties of the same thing each season, such as swimsuits and shoes, whereas I could get by with the same swimsuit and shoes for years, assuming Kim wouldn't eventually refuse to be seen with me.

Regarding larger financial outlays, I wouldn't be averse to buying the newest powerful computer system every couple of years, but Kim would say, "How powerful a computer do you need?" That's hard to argue with, particularly when you haven't even used your money-tracking software until this year. And then there is the use of credit cards. One of us rather likes them, one of us unequivocally does not. And neither is the one whom you might expect. Tradition has it that Wife is most likely to be seen galloping off with the rallying cry, "Charge!" But in our case, I confess, it is Husband. I don't mean I have a penchant for going into frivolous debt, but it doesn't bother me in the least to hand over my MasterVisaDiscoverCard for all manner of purchases. To watch Kim hesitantly pull out a credit card from her purse, by contrast, you'd think she was yanking out her own molars.

I see her point, but try occasionally to persuade her

that credit cards aren't all bad. They're essential for traveling, of course, and handy for emergencies such as when I'm short of cash and really *need* to make that lifesaving visit to Starbucks. Or when we're forced to charge our car repair bills in order to drive to work in order to make enough money in order to pay our car repair charges. And then there was the time that a credit card truly saved my posterior when I used it (the card) to jimmy open a window latch after locking myself out of our house.

But all joking aside, my wife has the right idea. We should all have such a problem pulling out our credit cards, given the alarming levels of consumer debt that plague our age. Sometimes Jesus' statement that you can't serve God and money seems a little abstract, but here is one place where it comes into sharp focus. There's a common maxim that goes, "Live simply so others can simply live." Perhaps a contrasting saying would be, "Spend lavishly and you are truly spent."

Leading My Life

From time to time my wife and I will collapse on the sofa late in the evening and grumble that often-repeated lament, "We're not leading our lives, our lives are leading us." Every day responsibilities stack on responsibilities, seemingly without our knowledge or consent.

For a long time I took a little comfort in the fact that we couldn't help any of this. Or so I thought. But then I read the sobering reflections of another calendar-challenged person, who took a hard look at her maddeningly hectic, messy, complicated life and concluded, "I really have no one to blame but myself."

It got me thinking about my own penchant for blaming busyness on circumstances beyond my control. I began to imagine a conversation I might have one day with the frayed and frazzled entity that is "my life"…

At a social gathering, possibly the birthday of my wife's second cousin or my second cousin's wife—or was it my cousin's second wife?—I was chatting a bit with a distant relative whom I hadn't seen for several years.

"So Phil," the relative inquired, "have you been busy lately?"

"Too busy, Bill," I said with a smirk. "You know what they say. I'm not leading my life so much as my life is leading me."

"I resent that," came the reply.

"Oh, sorry Bill," I said. "I wasn't meaning to offend…"

Bill was looking at me strangely. "What do you mean offend?" he asked. "I was just standing here nodding."

That's when I noticed the full length mirror behind Bill with my own reflection glaring back at me. I hadn't realized my expression was so surly. It rendered me speechless for a moment.

"Uh, you OK Phil?" Bill inquired.

"Ha ha," I said, a little more maniacally than I'd intended. "My reflection in that mirror there just gave me a start."

Bill looked around and frankly seemed a bit pale when he turned back to me. "Mirror?" he inquired weakly, inching toward the dining room. That's when I was stunned to realize there was no mirror at all, only someone standing there who looked exactly like me. My astonishment at meeting a look-alike relative was quickly overcome, however, by irritation at the rude glare he was giving me.

"Do I know you?" I snapped.

"Just Bill, the not-contractor," squeaked Bill as he exited the living room at lightning speed, leaving his glass of soda spinning in mid-air.

"Do you know me?" the look-alike growled. "Just look in a mirror."

I almost laughed maniacally again, but caught myself. "Fun-nee. What's your problem, anyway?"

"What you said."

"What I said?"

"Ha!" the twin barked. "I figured you didn't know what you were talking about."

"I don't know what you're talking about!" I blurted before realizing how dumb it sounded.

The look-alike explained, "You said 'I'm not leading my life, my life is leading me.' It is, in fact, the fifth time you've said it this week. Well, I'm pretty fed up with it. I demand you quit blaming me for your problems."

"And who exactly *are* you?"

"The one you keep claiming is leading you," the twin said. "I'm your life."

Suddenly I felt dizzy and had to sit down a moment. That's when I realized, sprawled on the carpet, that I

should have found a chair to sit on. People were star-
ing. So I stood up and scuttled my scowling twin into
an empty bedroom.

"Where do you get off treating me like that?" I scolded.

"That's what I wanted to ask you," he replied.
"You're wearing me out!"

I had to admit the guy did look bedraggled. Hair a
bit mussed, circles under his eyes and a distinct aura of
exasperation about him. Suddenly I felt sorry for him.
"Looks like you could use some rest," I offered.
"Maybe you should go home and go to bed."

Well, that really set him off. You could practically see
steam shooting out of his ears. "You just don't get it,
do you? I'm your life! If you don't go to bed, I don't go
to bed. If you don't slow down, I don't slow down. If
you don't relax, I don't relax. Can't you see you're running us ragged?"

This was sounding pretty weird, but from the looks
of him I figured I'd better go along with it. "It's not my
fault," I said. "Life is just too busy these days."

"There you go blaming me again. But listen, pal,
you've got no one to blame but yourself."

"How can you say that?" I asked, pulling out my
pocket calendar and flipping the pages. "Look at this.
Every day packed to the margins. If it was up to me, I
wouldn't schedule myself so silly."

"Ah," my twin said with a smirk. "So somebody's
been stealing your calendar and writing appointments
in it, eh?"

"Of course not, but I..."

"Then the writing must appear magically while you're
sleeping."

"That's silly, but let me..."

"Calendar virus?"

"Now see here..."

"You mean to tell me," the twin exclaimed with a
shocked expression, "that you've been penciling in all
those things yourself?"

"Well yes, but..."

"Then I don't see how you can slide the responsibility off on someone else. You, and you alone, are the one scheduling yourself silly."

I opened my mouth to say something, but there was nothing in there to say. The twin took advantage of the lull and pulled me over to the bedroom mirror. "See?" he said. "This is what you're doing to us."

I looked in the mirror...and got quite a jolt. I was he! Messy hair, baggy eyes, the whole bedraggled appearance. Then I whirled around to discover that "he" was gone.

At that point everything got foggy, and it slowly dawned on me that someone was patting my hand and inquiring, "Phil? Phil? You all right?"

It was my wife. I blinked a few times and noticed I was lying on a bed. "What happened?" I asked.

"You weren't feeling well and we said you should lie down," Kim replied. "Should I call the doctor?"

"Is my life still here?" I inquired, and realized when Kim gave me a funny look that perhaps it was a rather strange thing to say. So I added a quick laugh and joked, "I mean, am I still alive?"

Kim seemed worried that I was acting odd (even for me) and said maybe we *should* call the doctor, but I assured her that everything was OK. By now I realized it was all a dream. Whew. I sat up, took inventory of myself and said, "Guess I'm over-tired from being too busy lately."

"I've been concerned about that," Kim said. "Let's go home and get you to bed."

As we made our way to the car, I commented, "Think I'll cancel tomorrow's appointments and rest up a little. No sense in leading my life right into the hospital."

At that point I'm sure I heard a voice whisper in my ear, "Amen to that, brother." But there was no way I was going to look around to see who it was.

PART FIVE

Guys and Gals

Time to Relapse

How Do We Spell Relax?
SPROING!

I was very much taken with a passing comment my young nephew made one Sunday a few summers ago. Various family members had gathered at my parents' house for dinner, and now the adults were lounging and visiting. The nephew in question blustered in from a beautiful afternoon, which the other kids were enjoying outside, and flopped on the carpet complaining, "There's nothing to do."

My response was not to roll my eyes or mutter, "Kids today," as is generally the fashion. I remember distinctly, almost audibly thinking, "Nothing to do? I wish *I* had nothing to do!"

During that time in my life, it seemed like I had everything to do. I was a fairly new father, still trying to figure out the parenting scene. I'd also taken on some new job responsibilities that had me working extra hours. At church we were carrying out a number of fresh vision and organizational items with the worship team. These were all good things, but the pleasing possibility of ever again flopping anywhere and sighing, "I have nothing to do," seemed remote and even laughable.

Later I got to thinking that even in less busy times, my wife and I are not very good at doing nothing. I've come to realize this may be more serious than it sounds. One Bible verse I particularly like is Psalm 127:2: "It is senseless for you to work so hard from early morning until late at night...for God wants his loved ones to get their proper rest" (TLB). Yet I've rarely taken those words seriously enough. Rest is something to do if there's time at the end of the day or week—and there usually isn't.

When evening comes we do generally try to make

space for relaxation, but often at that point we seem to discover springs in our back pockets. I will attempt, say, to settle on the sofa with a good book, and *sproing*, I pop right back up to roll the garbage bin out, having just remembered that tomorrow is trash day. I come back in to stretch out with my book, and *sproing*, I'm quickly up again when it occurs to me that I haven't yet sent that e-mail message a colleague still needs tonight. Once more I return to the sofa, pausing a moment to satisfy myself that there's nothing else I forgot, and sit down to *sproing*, jump up and attend to one of my children who has wandered sleepily out for a drink of water.

Meanwhile my wife has also begun to make her way over, book in hand, to settle in for the evening. Just as denim is about to meet sofa cushion, the phone rings and *sproing*, Kim jumps up to answer it. She comes with phone back to the sofa, but as knees are bending *sproing*, she must run off for pen and paper to write down a message. Still talking, she returns and attempts to sit down once more—slowly and cautiously this time—and of course once more must *sproing* to retrieve her planning calendar to check a date.

As for me, I have returned from watering my child and am easing down onto the sofa slowly like a shortstop ready to snag a line drive. Sure enough, *sproing*, the dryer buzzer goes off. As I empty and fold clothes I'm sure I can hear the dryer snickering at me. Eventually I go back to the sofa and *sproing*, realize I've left my book in the laundry room, much to the dryer's guffawing delight. With book in hand and a dim glimmer of hope that now, finally, I can take a load off, *sproing*, it's time to get up and go to bed!

The backyard hammock seems similarly resistant to our efforts to relax, but with the hammock we rarely even make it to *sproing*. We always look forward to the day when the weather warms up and dries out enough to string the hammock up between two apple trees.

Climbing on to test the knots, I always make poetic plans: *Ahh, it will be nice to lie out here summer evenings, swaying in the breeze and gazing at the sky through green leafy branches.* But in reality, my most intimate acquaintance with the hammock the rest of spring and summer will likely be the quick glances I give it while rushing past with lawn mower or hedge clippers. *It'll sure feel good to lie down on that when the work is done,* I'll think, *say in about 25 years.*

Mostly it's my own fault. While it's true that we live in a busy time that is less conducive to the extended use of hammocks and sofas, it's equally true that I don't have a restful nature. A few years ago Kim handed me a cartoon clipped out of a magazine and said, "That's you." It depicted a man standing stiffly on a living room chair, his fists clenched and eyes bugged out. The man's wife is telling her friend, "Harold has never quite learned how to relax."

Too often, that *is* me. I have often been puzzled how a memory that's so unreliable during the day—I routinely misplace keys, notes, files, thoughts—can become so thoroughly photographic at night. As soon as I sit down to relax, all the little things I forgot suddenly clamor for attention. All the things to fix and file and delegate and do decide to badger me until *sproing,* I'm up trying to tackle everything at once.

Part of the problem is that I'm a natural born worrier. I still remember vividly one Monday morning in first grade when I forgot to bring my milk money for the week. My teacher practically had a nervous breakdown about it. She was probably just having a bad day, as adults tend to do, but in those days I hadn't yet fathomed that teachers were real people rather than robots or types of classroom furniture.

So my teacher's anxiety made me think I'd committed some kind of monumental gaffe. Forgetting my milk money! The poor people at the dairy we'd visited on a field trip the previous week might go broke. Other dairies could be hurt. It would cause a ripple effect throughout the farming industry. American agribusiness would go into decline. The entire world would suffer. All caused by the silly boy who forgot his milk money!

I'll admit I had an overactive imagination, and would like to say that I grew out of such morbid fascination with my role in global destruction. But unfortunately I didn't. My mind can still conjure monumental disasters from minor oversights. Which is one reason why, when I try to settle on sofa or hammock, I have a hard time leaving well enough alone. Something needs doing somewhere. If I don't do it, who will?

Sometimes the correct answer to that, I've been trying to tell myself more often, is "Nobody." Not everything has to get done right this minute. It's one of a number of lessons I've been learning about how to relax. A few others are...

• **My "To Do" list wasn't brought down from the mountain by Moses.** The problem I have with To Do lists is that I can't quite rest until I get to the end of one—but I can never seem to get to the end of one. Something compels me not only to keep adding to the list, but also to regard it as some kind of sacred transcription that must be followed to the letter.

Yet it always amazes me that I can so studiously prepare an iron-clad, divinely-inspired To Do list prior to a trip—things that *absolutely must* get done before leaving the office—and never even get through half of it. And what happens when all those critical things on my list don't get done? Nothing. Most of the time nobody even notices. Perhaps some of these items weren't as vitally important to the survival of the universe as I thought.

• **I'm not performing surgery.** No doubt it would be somewhat frowned upon for a surgeon, in the middle of open-heart surgery, to holler "Quittin' time!" and suggest that everyone get back to it first thing in the morning. I, however, am not a surgeon. It is perfectly acceptable for me to come back to my work later.

In theory.   In practice, I have a hard time laying down the tools of my trade during an open document. When I realize, however, that nobody's life will be endangered by my failure to finish a sentence or paragraph just this minute, it gets a little easier to relax.

• **It doesn't all have to be brilliant.** There are some things, such as my marriage and my spiritual life, that call for my absolute, 100% best efforts. There are some things, such as my golf game or the fortunes of my favorite sports team, that do not. People today seem to have difficulty with that. We work at our play, as someone said, and play at our work. We spend far too much time and effort on things that don't matter, and far too little on things that do.

When I remember that I'd rather have, for example, an above-par marriage than a below-par golf game, it inspires me to ease up a bit on things that aren't so important.

• **God wasn't kidding about getting some rest.** When God instituted the original Sabbath, not only did he tell the people to take a day off, he said that those who didn't would be put to death.   Initially we might smirk at such an antiquated notion or breathe a sigh of relief that we no longer live under such a threat. But in our rest-deprived age, God's largely ignored Sabbath intentions may need reviewing and renewing.

The point of Sabbath was not that God could throw around His weight with humans, but that humans wouldn't throw around their weight with each other. Biblical rest was all about restoring relationships. Take a weekly break from making a profit, trying to get your own, looking out for number one. Honor God, enjoy your family, live at peace with others.

Perhaps the reason these kinds of activities seem so remote and unfathomable today is because we can barely even relax for an hour. God may want His loved ones to get their proper rest—but not on our time, thank you.

Keeping Up the Castle

Some may say it's sexist to claim that "A man's home is his castle," but after owning my own castle for a number of years, I wouldn't necessarily encourage women everywhere to lobby for equal castle rights. Frankly, castles can be a pretty big pain in the moat.

When my wife and I viewed our current castle before purchasing it, for instance, it was evident that the former Lord and Lady weren't big on castle maintenance. The place needed some work. But we bought it anyway, because first, we thought a fixer-upper would be a better value for our money; second, we thought fixing up a fixer-upper in our spare time would be kind of fun; and third, we were completely out of our minds. As naive first-time homeowners, we just didn't realize how much time and effort it really took to fix a fixer-upper up.

The kitchen cabinets, for example, suffered from rusty hardware and an explosive shade of yellow that could most favorably be viewed from interstellar space. One of our first evening's home-improvement jobs after we moved in, then, would be to replace the hardware, sand the cabinets and paint them antique white. Perhaps experienced home improvers can already spot a fatal flaw in our thinking. Of course the job took much longer than an evening.

First, I removed all the old hinges and handles in about 30 minutes. So far so good. Then I power-sanded the doors and woodwork in another hour or so. No problem. Now, I began to mount the new hinges. Problem. About the fifth screw in, I broke off a screwhead with my power driver. After a bit of terse reflection about the chintzyness of the screws and how they didn't make things like they used to, I was forced to painstakingly remove the broken screw with a needlenose pliers and fetch a coffee can marked "Misc." to rummage around for a new screw.

Another problem. My finger came up bleeding from an uncovered razor blade thoughtlessly thrown in the can by someone I could have just given a piece of my mind...oh, I guess it was me. More grim mumbling as I bandaged my finger in the bathroom. Then I resumed my rummaging for an appropriate screw, much more carefully this time, and went back to work. Until the next screw-head broke off, and I was forced once more to take up the pliers and go to the can (coffee, I mean). These steps repeated themselves a number of times until I finally got the new hinges in place—fortunately with only a few fingers bandaged and my power driver still in hand, rather than out in the yard, where it might have been hurled through a window had I broken off one more screw.

Despite the hinge delay that got me rather unhinged, I managed at length to take up a brush and assist my wife, who had begun laying on a coat of antique white. Much later than anticipated, we finished the work and stumbled off to bed. In the morning we stumbled back to view the results, at which point we discovered to our dismay that the cabinets were still Hydrogen Yellow.

Or so they seemed. The paint hadn't covered well at all, causing us to regret our decision to forego using primer to save steps. Needless to say, we had to spend the next several evenings bullying the cabinets into staying white by brushing on several more coats of paint.

This, we found out, was what home improvement was all about. Trial and error, tenacity and perseverance. Almost every project took far longer than we anticipated. We did manage to get most of the major work done on our house in the first few years, but smaller projects linger on, now into year nine. And the amazing thing, the truly astonishing thing, is that the moment we finish the last updates and details and touch-ups, we will likely sell this house and buy a bigger fix-er-upper to fix up. Yes, keeping up our castle has driven us completely crackers.

Another aspect of castle-maintenance that has tried our patience from time to time has been figuring out where everything goes. Though someone has said that you can't have everything—where would you put it?—sometimes it seems as if we have *almost* everything. When my wife and I moved from our smaller rental house to our current place, it didn't occur to us that storage might be a problem. But we accumulated various household items and yard implements, not to mention a couple of children, and eventually the drawers and closets and garage seemed to overflow. We'd like to pass it off as one of the inevitable hazards of home-ownership, but realize it's just another hassle we've brought on ourselves.

Recently in the garage I came across an old-time crank hand drill, for example, that I've never used in my life. So why do I keep it around? I might need it, of course. That's why I bought it for a buck at a garage sale—to use in those situations where hand drills are just the thing. Not that I could think of any at the time, but surely something would come up. So I paid my dollar and years later the thing still takes up space, waiting for me to drill something. But I'm not really going to pass up the modern convenience of my power drill in favor of a cranky old contraption with lousy aim.

And so it goes for an assortment of other dubiously useful stuff we can't quite bring ourselves to get rid of. Among other things, our garage harbors a wing chair Kim may or may not recover someday, a couple of old dining room chairs I may or may not refinish someday, a box of old record albums that have nostalgic value but no actual record player to play them, and a large storage cabinet with sliding doors waiting for shelves to be installed so we can store things like old unplayable record albums.

Certainly there are many people who don't have this problem, who have a place for everything and everything in its place. There are others of us, though, who struggle with today's cluttered culture, in which we tend to collect extras of everything.

One evening a few years ago I became bemused with the fact that we owned three separate remote control units—one for the TV, one for the VCR, and one for the stereo. It seemed like Kim and I were forever searching for one of them. Especially at that time when our children were young and prone to wandering off with things, the question occurred to me: Where is the proper place to store a TV remote? In a drawer? No, because at our house drawers apparently contained internal transmogrifyers that beamed whatever we put in them elsewhere so that items were never in the right drawer (or any drawer) when we looked for them. On the table beside the sofa? No, because our children might get hold of the remote and put it somewhere convenient for them but inconvenient for us, such as in the backyard sandbox. On top of the TV? No, because after a long day when we'd collapse on the sofa to watch something, there the remote would be, sitting on top of the TV snickering at us. And neither of us would have the energy to get up and fetch it.

But in reality, we shouldn't watch TV anyway. We should look around, take stock of home maintenance items that need attending to, and review our A to Zs of keeping up the castle. Tonight, I think we'll start with zzzzzzzz. . .

Finding the Perfect Life

Kim and I decided that we were tired of wearing ourselves out on demanding jobs, challenging family issues, ongoing relationship concerns, frustrating church conflicts and insidious home upkeep. So we decided to acquire a perfect life. There were plenty of varieties to choose from. Every day any number of organizations, publications and advertisers could be seen trotting out their perfect-life wares. The trick would be finding the perfect life that would prove perfect for us.

One popular model that many churches and politicians were pushing was the 1950s, with its clean living, faultless families and cars the size of river barges. We decided to check into it. This wasn't difficult, since cable TV was packed with '50s sitcoms that traditional-family valuists were always going on about. After watching several hours of *Ozzie and Harriet, Leave It To Beaver* and *Father Knows Best,* we sat down for a meeting. I asked Kim, "What do you think? Is that our perfect life?"

"I'm impressed with how clean the houses are," Kim said, "though I'm a little concerned about how they got that way."

"Maybe they have servants," I ventured.

"I think they do," Kim replied. "Their wives."

"*Touché,*" I said. "But you have to admit that the children are polite. Even the teens never said anything sassier than 'gosh.' Our eight-year-old would scare the pants off those kids."

"Yes, they are polite," Kim agreed. "Very nice. Quite well behaved. Kind of boring."

"I suppose. And Dad sure sat around a lot after work wearing a cardigan and wingtips. Didn't he ever get out and play basketball or go in-line skating with the kids?"

"I guess the '50s were all right in the '50s," Kim said, "but I doubt they'd be right for us. What other kind of perfect life could we get?"

After some discussion, we agreed that the relaxed *Country Living* scenario had excellent potential as an antidote for our stressed-out existence. Kim called up some country-dwelling friends to probe into the perfection level of their lifestyle and she came back with news. "They're heading out of town for a week and said they'd be happy to have us house-sit for them. That way we can experience country life firsthand."

Perfect. We got to their place at dusk one evening and were immediately enchanted. A beautiful sunset hovered over the verdant hills. The old farmhouse stood picturesquely before us. We went in and quickly felt at home among the wonderfully restored antique furnishings right out of *House Beautiful.*

Kim and I grinned a perfect grin that lasted until, oh, about ten minutes after we went to bed, when an awful racket from the bowels of the house jolted us upright. I grabbed a shoe (figuring if it was a burglar or bear I could at least odorize them into submission) and went cautiously to investigate. Soon I returned to report, "Just the old furnace rattling in the basement. Looks like a space alien down there."

We went back to sleep for, oh, another ten minutes, at which point an owl started hooting mightily outside the window. I never knew those things could hoot so loud—they had always seemed rather quiet in cartoons. And in fact as the night wore on we became more and more annoyed that the quiet countryside kept being so infernally noisy. The old house creaked, the furnace rasped, frogs croaked, crickets chirped, farm animals bleated, until the moment, about the time we finally drifted off to sleep, when the neighbor's rooster practically crowed us through the ceiling.

"We'll probably get used to it," we assured each other at the breakfast table, both of us rubbing our eyes and guzzling coffee. And Kim doesn't even drink coffee. But she needed it to stay awake during the 30 mile drive into town to deliver the kids to school and go to work—a commute she later said wasn't entirely bad, if you didn't count the 20 minute sheep crossing and meteor-crater potholes. Fortunately my commute consisted merely of hooking up my computer and observing, as the screen flickered to life, the electricity go out. Great.

With a flashlight I found the ancient, many-eyed fuse box in the basement near the alien heater, but there didn't appear to be any fuses blown. So I headed back up to call our friends at the number they'd left. The phone was down too. Good thing I had my cell phone, which helpfully flashed, "No service." Great. Finally I did find service on a little hill after trudging around the countryside for an hour, and thankfully was able to get through. "Your power is out," I said, "and your phone. What should I do?"

"Cow probably knocked over the power pole again," my friend replied. "They usually get it fixed in a day or two." *Great.*

Needless to say, after a week of poor sleep, sheepy commutes, intermittent power and trudging several times a day to the little cell-phoning hill, we were itching (literally with all that poison oak around) to get back home.

"Bet you're glad to be back!" we said to our friends when they pulled up.

"Not really," they replied. "The reason we were gone was to purchase a condo in Portland. Country life was wearing us out. Wanna buy our place?"

Not a chance. Mellow country living was far too stressful for us.

Scratching our way home, Kim commented, "Maybe we're being too materialistic in our search for perfection. Maybe we should take more of a spiritual approach."

Excellent thought. There was a nice little perfect-life

package to be found, after all, in the Contemporary Christian ideal, which combined a flawless spirituality with an attractive consumer lifestyle. We'd always steered a bit clear of the Health and Wealth gospel before, but maybe we were taking Jesus too seriously when he said, "You cannot serve both God and Money." Ha ha—the kidder.

So we joined a big-name church with celebrity pastors and worship leaders, a national TV audience prone to sending in truckloads of cash, and a food court complete with espresso bar. Heaven already. The congregation was beautiful and affluent, the music hip and poppy, and the sermons smooth and easy to swallow— nothing too tough to chew on or too demanding to think about beyond Sunday noon. Best of all, our children disappeared into their own amusement-park wing of the church, never to cross paths with us again until we were ready to go home to our tasteful, upper-middle class, white Christian neighborhood. Needless to say, all was bliss.

For awhile. One day while we were driving along our perfect street with our perfect kids, on the way home to our perfect house on another perfect Sunday, Kim suddenly looked over at me and blurted, "I miss our old house."

"That broken-down thing?" I asked. "How could you miss it?"

"It had character," Kim said. "Sometimes in our perfect house I want to throw the artfully arranged sofa pillows on the floor and knock the tasteful Scripture placards off the walls, but of course they're all super-glued in place."

"Now that you mention it," I mused, "I kind of miss my old job. It had too many deadlines, not enough perks and was mostly a major headache. I sort of liked that. Added spice to the day."

"I miss my old friends," Kim added. "Sure they could get on my nerves, but the nice thing was, I could also get on theirs. Then we could laugh about it. We knew we weren't perfect, but it was OK. Not as much pressure."

"Speaking of which, I miss our old kids," I said. "They were wiggly and whiny and messy and unpredictable and aggravating and asked all kinds of hard questions that made my eyes bug out. It was great."

"I even miss our old church," Kim declared. "It may not have been trendy or hip or cutting-edge, but there was something real about it. Down to earth. Sometimes I wonder if this Contemporary Christian ideal is just too good to be true."

"Maybe we got so caught up in finding the perfect life," I mused, "we failed to appreciate what we already had. Do you think we should have stuck with our old life?"

Kim nodded. "Now that," she said, "was perfect."

Just Desserts For Me, Thanks

I arrived at the airport early one morning to catch my plane, only to discover that the departure time had been delayed. So I scurried over to the coffee bar for a mocha. The line was fairly long, but I stepped in to shuffle forward with the other groggy business travelers. A few moments later a couple of self-important-looking men bulled past and blared, "Coming through! We're stockholders in this coffee franchise."

Well la-de-da. As they cut in at the front of the line and ordered *lattes*, the rest of us were too stunned or too polite or both to send them to the back of the line, perhaps with some motivation from the sole. The woman in front of me summed up all of our feelings well, though, when she growled under her breath, "Who do they think *they* are?"

So it was with a certain—no, I would say an *extreme* amount of pleasure that we witnessed what followed. As the smug stockholders swooped over to grab their *lattes* from the pick-up counter, one of them mis-timed his grab and knocked the drinks over, liberally splashing himself, his luggage and the other guy with nasty brown stains. I can't say I had ever seen justice served so quickly and satisfyingly. It was only with a great amount of effort, I think, that we onlookers refrained from bursting into spontaneous applause.

On the plane I kept thinking about that incident. What if all infractions against common courtesy, most of which go tragically unpunished, met such swift and just desserts? It was a delicious scenario to contemplate...

• At the grocery store, someone is wheeling toward the only open checker with a gravity-defying heap of groceries and a wad of what looks to be about 100 coupons. When they notice you are also approaching with a single carton of milk, they speed up to make sure they get to the checker before you.

Just desserts: They wheel their groceries out to discover that a bread truck has parked directly behind their car and they can't back out. Upon looking for the driver they discover a note on the window that says, "Out to lunch. Back in an hour."

• Someone drives back and forth in front of your house several times a day playing a huge thumping stereo loud enough to vibrate your windows, interrupt your phone conversations, wake the baby and significantly raise your blood pressure.

Just desserts: A Barry Manilow album gets stuck in the thumper's CD tray and no one can figure out how to turn it off.

• Certain middle-aged, out of shape guys approach a basketball or softball league with delusions that first, they are good, and second, winning will actually make a difference in the universal scheme of things. Thus they feel free to yell at umpires, order other players around and generally make each game a miserable experience.

Just desserts: Sprained ankles, out for the season.

• One of those drivers who assumes they are above the traffic laws whips her fancy BMW past you and cuts you off, then proceeds to weave in and out of traffic, pass semi-trucks on curves and put everyone else on the road at risk.

Just desserts: She has a breakdown in the middle of nowhere and gets towed to Bubba's Auto Shop, whose only loaner vehicle is a rusting VW Bus that refuses to shift above second gear.

• A thoughtful pet owner allows pooping in your yard without bothering to clean up.

Just desserts: Pet owner would go home to find that his sewer has backed up and gifted him with a bit of aromatic cleanup of his own.

• Advertisers insult viewers' intelligence by implying that laundry soap, for example, can change your life.

Just desserts: These advertisers would accidentally lock themselves in a room with nothing to watch but their own commercials.

• A church member complains to everyone in sight about the lack of a program or ministry they think should obviously be happening.

Just desserts: The complaining member would be put in immediate charge of developing the missing program or ministry, no questions asked.

I could go on, of course. The Just Desserts principle has endless possibilities. Which is also what worries me. If everyone actually got what they deserved, wouldn't that include me? Because, hard as it may be to believe, I have occasionally committed crimes against common courtesy too...

• I'm working after hours, during the time I always go on about setting aside for "family time," when my son comes in and asks if we can play a game or build something with Legos. I reply, "Not tonight son, I'm a busy man."

Just desserts: The next evening when I knock on Seth's door and ask him to play, he says, "Not tonight Dad, I'm a busy man."

• I complain heartily when my fast-food seems to take longer than it should, when bank service seems a bit slow, when something doesn't arrive in the mail fast enough, or when other small things seem to be causing a big waste of my precious time.

Just desserts: Every time I show up late for an appointment or a meeting (which is far too often), everyone takes me to task for causing a big waste of their precious time.

• I fail to say, "I love you" to my wife every day, because after all these years of being married, she should just *know* I love her without having to say it.

Just desserts: My wife decides not to make dinner on

her night to cook, because after all these years of eating, I should just *know* what dinner tastes like without having to consume it.

• I look down on someone for failing to meet my moral standards, or refuse someone charity because I think they don't deserve it.

Just desserts: During my prayer time God tells me, "Sorry, you didn't meet my moral standards today and don't deserve my grace anyway, so I'm not going to acknowledge your existence anymore."

That makes me think this Just Desserts concept isn't such a good idea after all. Admittedly there is a certain guilty pleasure in imagining swift and decisive consequences for all courtesy violators, such as the butting-in coffee bar guys who got splattered with what they deserved. But I wouldn't want it happening to *me*.

Doing (In) Our Devotions

There's an old joke about a man who uses the "flip and point" method for daily devotions. One morning in his usual rush between breakfast and work, he hastily flips open his Bible and randomly points to Matthew 27:5: "So Judas went away and hanged himself." Alarmed, he flips again and points to Luke 10:37: "Go and do likewise."

That man, of course, was me.

Well, maybe not literally, but I have been known to flip and point a few times myself. Which has more than a little to do, I think, with the big rush I seem to be in all the time. With so many important matters to attend to, such as receiving critical e-mail messages containing knock-knock jokes, who has time for trivial stuff like devotions?

Of course I don't really think reading e-mail humor is more important than doing devotions, but the contrast illustrates how easily the minutiae of modern living can squeeze out more weighty matters. Most of us would likely agree that devotions—taking time for daily Bible study, reflection and prayer—are one of the most important activities a person can engage in. So important, in fact, that we regularly forget or neglect to do it.

But I don't think we mean to. My wife and I, who often struggle with doing devotions ourselves, have noticed several things that seem to make the whole project more daunting. First, life is busy. This may seem rather obvious. But more than ever in our hectic age, what we have to do (attend meetings, fold laundry, shuttle kids to practice) tends to supersede what we intend to do (exercise, do devotions, read books). And in what little discretionary time is left, what is easier to do (watch TV, sleep 20 more minutes) often displaces what is hard to do. Which leads to the second point...

Devotions are difficult. However much contemporary Christianity would like to make everything spiritual as streamlined and easy to swallow as possible, reading Scripture, reflecting on life and faith, and spending time in prayer are formidable endeavors. And doing them makes certain demands on us. Following God's word and praying "Thy will be done" may mean we have to change. Along with that difficulty, a third point is...

Devotions don't always produce immediate or measurable results. In a day when we stick cards into machines to get cash and think a five-minute wait at Taco Bell is too long, doing devotions can seem confoundingly unproductive. Here again many modern Christians uphold a "name it and claim it" philosophy that insists Scripture and prayer *always* produce tangible blessings and miracles (if you have enough faith). But mostly it doesn't happen like that. More often faith is a "pilgrimage" in the truest sense of the word—it takes patience, perseverance, tenacity and a willingness to press on through the occasional wilderness.

It's the difficulty of doing devotions, I think, that has produced a full marketplace of devotional gimmicks—or should I say "helps." A few years ago I was amazed to realize we had accumulated at least a half dozen study Bibles at our house. These are the Bibles packed with handy notes and quick interpretations geared to various target audiences. To name just a few varieties I've seen, there are men's study Bibles, women's study Bibles, couple's study Bibles, family study Bibles, teen study Bibles, children's study Bibles, worship study Bibles, renewal study Bibles, study Bibles in various translations, study Bibles sanctioned by big-name para-church movements, and so on. Not that I have anything against study Bibles, but I have wondered if taking the work out of Bible study is really such a good thing.

After discovering our overabundance of study Bibles,

in fact, I worried about relying too much on "prefab" interpretations and decided to get back to basic, unadorned Scripture. So I shelved the tattered old NIV model I'd been lugging around for years and went to purchase a slimmer Bible with no notes or cross references. I found what I was looking for—in a "clearance" bin.

While I appreciated getting a reduced price, the fact that basic Bibles were being cleared out troubled me. Had study Bibles completely taken over the regular shelves? I began to imagine a conversation I might have had with the bookstore clerk...

Me: "I'm looking for a Bible."

Clerk: "Very good. And what variety would you like: the Men's, Husband's, Dad's, Single's, Single Dad's, Ex-Husband's, Employee's, Employer's, Churchgoer's, Occasional Churchgoer's, Sports Lover's, Web Surfer's, or Couch Potato's Study Bible?"

Me: "Um, don't you have any regular Bibles?"

Clerk: "Regular? What do you mean?"

Me: "You know, just the Bible. Nothing with 'Study' in the title."

Clerk: "Ha ha, good one. Now, we also have the Golfer's, Gardener's, Woodworker's, Softball Player's..."

It's not that I'm against study Bibles, as I've mentioned, or other trendy Scripture formats. Some of them have been a great help in our home. My wife and I both carried NIV Study Bibles for a long time before she, too, recently shelved hers in favor of a smaller non-study Bible. We also benefited awhile back from reading through the popular One-Year Bible, which we finished in only two years and three months. We've also used and enjoyed various devotional guides and passage-a-day calendars. And I doubt I could even manage anymore without my Bible software, which saves me from the exhaustion of pulling out that massive old *Strong's Exhaustive Concordance.*

Given the modern tendency to make faith and spirituality as easy and painless as possible, however, I sometimes feel concern about where devotional trends might be heading. I can just imagine what some high-tech, cutting edge devotional aids might look like in the future:

• **Wrist Bible.** This would strap on the wrist like a digital watch and contain the entire Bible at the push of a button. It would also have a biorhythm sensor so that at appropriate times of the day the most needed verse for how one is feeling would flash on the screen.

If you're dragging a bit in the morning, for instance, Psalm 98:1 might come up: "Sing to the LORD a new song, for he has done marvelous things." There you go. Six seconds, and your custom devotional moment is done. But perhaps by mid-morning the moment has worn off, and you're feeling a bit frustrated with the work that's piling up. Philippians 4:6 could then flash on the screen: "Do not be anxious about anything." Notice how the second part of the sentence, "Pray about everything," has been helpfully left off. That way you can move right on without actually having to pray.

By afternoon, though, an obnoxious colleague might be getting on your nerves. Sensing this, the Wrist Bible might call up Psalm 3:7: "O my God! Strike all my enemies on the jaw; break the teeth of the wicked." Wouldn't you feel better? The inspiration would likely carry you all the way through the evening, until the time you settle on the sofa to visit with your spouse. That's when the Wrist Bible could flash Song of Solomon 7:6: "How beautiful you are and how pleasing, O love, with your delights!" But then your spouse's wrist Bible might retort with Exodus 32:10: "Now leave me alone so that my anger may burn." Perhaps some type of scrambler could be added so you can control what Scriptures appear on other people's wrist Bibles, too.

Another forward-thinking devotional method that would bypass the annoying need to manually open and read one's Bible would be...

• **Subliminal Scriptures.** Soft Scripture CDs set to the sound of soothing tropical breezes or smooth sea waves could be played during what many of us consider to be our most mentally superior time of day—while we're sleeping. Not only would they save the effort of trying to schedule devotional time each day, they could also greatly enhance one's spiritual reputation. When those irritating, devotionally committed folks comment about reading and praying a half-hour or an hour every day, Subliminal Scripture users could humbly observe that they spend *eight hours* a day in the Word.

For traditionalist who feel that devotions should be done while awake, though, another potential devotional method could be...

• **Personal Bible.** In many greeting-card stores today there is computer equipment set up to make personalized birthday and anniversary cards. A similar principle could be put to use in Bible Bookstores. People could print out their own personalized versions of the Bible, depending on their particular religious tastes. A few popular variations might be the SFV (Sin-Free Version), the BOV (Blessings-Only Version), the MMV (Make Money Version), the LWV (Lose Weight Version), the NVV (No Violence Version, expunging much of the Old Testament), the NHSV (No Hard Sayings Version, expunging much of the New Testament), and the TTV, (Top Ten Version, which reformats each book into a Top Ten List).

These kinds of futuristic devotional aids will probably never come about, of course. But I'm still convinced that we need to be careful about trying to simplify Bible study and prayer too much. Once during a time when I seemed to be particularly frustrated with the difference between what I wanted to happen and what was really happening (or not happening) in my devotional life, an intriguing insight occurred to me. Devotions weren't *supposed* to be easy, so why was I forever trying to make them that way? Grappling with the

Word, reflecting on my life, getting to know God better—these couldn't be dispatched in a few easy steps or a minimal number of minutes a day.

The same could be said for all our relationships. I've joked in this book about some of the assumptions we make and shortcuts we take in various aspects of our gender, family, church and other relations. However, there is a serious side to this modern desire for unlimited ease and comfort in all areas of life. We often want the rewards without the work, the blessings without the effort. We'd like to judge by appearances or trust popular opinion rather than getting to know someone or thinking something through ourselves. We want others to love, honor and esteem us without necessarily doing the same for them.

But relationships aren't supposed to be easy, so why do we try to make them that way? Strengthening our human and spiritual connections deserves our greatest pains and best efforts. No quick steps or surefire formulas can ever make it easier. Nor should they. In our haste to bypass the hard stuff these days, too often we end up missing the good stuff.

About the Author

P hil Wiebe has rich and varied experience in areas of writing, editing, and music. For nearly a decade his monthly *Christian Leader* column, "Ph'lip Side," has inspired readers both to smile and to think. Many national magazines have featured his articles and humor pieces, the latter having won several Evangelical Press Association awards. He also writes ad copy and professional documents for several organizations and businesses.

As an editor Phil directs publication of the inter-Mennonite devotional quarterly *Rejoice!,* and edits the *Word Wise* Bible study guide. He has also worked on the *Faith Family Focus* curriculum and various other projects.

For a number of years Phil toured professionally as a guitarist, songwriter, and singer with a widely-traveled contemporary Christian band. Currently he is a worship leader at Kingwood Bible Church (MB) in Salem, Oregon, where he enjoys life with wife Kim, son Seth, and daughter Madisen.